About Island Press

Since 1984, the nonprofit Island Press has been stimulating, shaping, and communicating the ideas that are essential for solving environmental problems worldwide. With more than 800 titles in print and some 40 new releases each year, we are the nation's leading publisher on environmental issues. We identify innovative thinkers and emerging trends in the environmental field. We work with world-renowned experts and authors to develop cross-disciplinary solutions to environmental challenges.

Island Press designs and implements coordinated book publication campaigns in order to communicate our critical messages in print, in person, and online using the latest technologies, programs, and the media. Our goal: to reach targeted audiences—scientists, policymakers, environmental advocates, the media, and concerned citizens—who can and will take action to protect the plants and animals that enrich our world, the ecosystems we need to survive, the water we drink, and the air we breathe.

Island Press gratefully acknowledges the support of its work by the Agua Fund, Inc., Annenberg Foundation, The Christensen Fund, The Nathan Cummings Foundation, The Geraldine R. Dodge Foundation, Doris Duke Charitable Foundation, The Educational Foundation of America, Betsy and Jesse Fink Foundation, The William and Flora Hewlett Foundation, The Kendeda Fund, The Andrew W. Mellon Foundation, The Curtis and Edith Munson Foundation, Oak Foundation, The Overbrook Foundation, the David and Lucile Packard Foundation, The Summit Fund of Washington, Trust for Architectural Easements, Wallace Global Fund, The Winslow Foundation, and other generous donors.

The opinions expressed in this book are those of the author(s) and do not necessarily reflect the views of our donors.

About Earthjustice

EARTHJUSTICE, the nation's largest public interest environmental law firm, has been fighting for years to preserve roadless public lands from abuse at the hands of governmental and private interests. It's a significant part of the organization's mission to protect the magnificent places, natural resources, and wildlife of the earth, and defend the right of all people to a healthy environment.

Earthjustice represents—without charge—hundreds of organizations, commercial and sport fishermen, scientists, outfitters, Native communities, and others. Most of the firm's work is in federal courts and before federal agencies, but it also deals at the state level and in other arenas. A true advocacy organization, Earthjustice augments its legal work with public information and education campaigns and public events.

Roadless Rules

The Struggle for the
Last Wild Forests

Roadless Rules

The Struggle for the Last Wild Forests

TOM TURNER

ISLAND PRESS / SHEARWATER BOOKS
Washington · Covelo · London

LIBRARY OF CONGRESS CATALOGING-IN-PUBLICATION DATA

Turner, Tom.
    Roadless rules : the struggle for the last wild forests / Tom Turner.
      p. cm.
    Includes bibliographical references.
    ISBN-13: 978-1-59726-439-6 (cloth : alk. paper)
    ISBN-10: 1-59726-439-3 (cloth : alk. paper)
    ISBN-13: 978-1-59726-440-2 (pbk. : alk. paper)
    ISBN-10: 1-59726-440-7 (pbk. : alk. paper) 1. Forest conservation—Government policy—United States—History. 2. Forest roads—Government policy—United States—History. 3. Forest policy—Government policy—United States—History. I. Title.
    SD412.T87 2009
    333.75'160973—dc22
    2008030849

 Printed on recycled, acid-free paper

Manufactured in the United States of America
10 9 8 7 6 5 4 3 2 1

Keywords: Roadless Area Conservation Rule, national forests, environmental campaign, Earthjustice, environmental law

Roads are the premier technology of empire, of centralization and homogenization . . . they are the literal avenues of conquest and colonialism. —STEPHANIE MILLS

As long as roads cut through wild country, they will hold the land vulnerable to future whims. The road running through this meadow is nothing more than a potholed portal for bad ideas, a puncture wound that won't heal, allowing human fallibility to flow unchecked into the delicate heart of healthy land. —GUY HAND

We now live in an America that is so vastly roaded and so thoroughly motorized that there is almost no place beyond easy reach of the recreational driver. —DAVID HAVLICK

Put roads into unroaded country and you sign a warrant of ill health or even death for numerous species. —TED KERASOTE

Where roads go, the life there in its million forms suffers, shrinks, pales, dies. —PHIL CONDON

Thanks to the interstate highway system, it is now possible to travel from coast to coast without seeing anything. —CHARLES KURALT

Contents

Acknowledgments

I AM GRATEFUL TO MANY PEOPLE for giving of their time and insights in helping me untangle this very complex story. First is Mike Dombeck, one of the heroes of the story, who was chief of the USDA Forest Service when the roadless rule was conceived and enacted. Dombeck's boss, Jim Lyons, was helpful and generous as well. Also Chris Wood, then a special advisor to Dombeck, later a staffer at Trout Unlimited and a key member of the Roadless Area Conservation National Advisory Committee. And Jim Furnish, whom Dombeck plucked from the Siuslaw National Forest in Oregon and brought to Washington to help shake up an inertia-bound bureaucracy.

On the other side of the issue is Mark Rey, Under Secretary of Agriculture for Natural Resources and Environment in the Bush administration, a former lobbyist for the timber industry, whom people in the environmental community tend to see as the arch villain. He was nonetheless gracious and helpful, knowing full well that I was affiliated with an organization that has sued him countless times, and I'm grateful for his consenting to an extensive interview. Much of what he says is disputed by partisans on the other side, of course, but I thought it only fair to give Mr. Rey free rein to express his views, which he was happy to do.

At its heart, this a story of the interplay between litigation and public policy, with plenty of politics and vast dollops of community organizing thrown in for good measure. From the conservation community I was greatly assisted by Mike Francis of The Wilderness Society, Mat Jacobson and Rob Vandermark of the Heritage Forests Campaign, Suellen Lowry of the Noah Alliance, Josh Reichert and Steve Kallick of the Pew Charitable Trusts Environment Group, Ken Rait of the Campaign for America's Wilderness, and Marty Hayden of Earthjustice.

The legal team that preserved the roadless rule through six-plus years of relentless attacks by industry and several states, working hand in hand with officials in the George W. Bush administration, includes Kristen Boyles, Todd True, Abigail Dillen, Deirdre McDonnell, Doug Honnold, Tim Preso, Jim Angell, and Tom Waldo of Earthjustice; Niel Lawrence of the Natural Resources Defense Council; Pat Parenteau of the Vermont Law School; and Claudia Polsky, an Earthjustice alumna now with the California Environmental Protection Agency. Heroes all, and all helpful.

I also wish to thank Peter Barnes and the Common Counsel Foundation, which run the Mesa Refuge at Point Reyes Station, California, where I was able to spend two quiet and productive weeks working on the early stages of the manuscript. Finally, I am grateful to Barbara Dean of Island Press, who was encouraging right from the start and offered many useful suggestions.

Introduction 1

ROADS ARE CENTRAL TO HUMAN CULTURE. We sing about roads ("Route 66," "On the Road to Mandalay," "Hit the Road, Jack," "The Coming of the Roads"). We write poems about roads ("The Road Not Taken," "The Silk Road"). We study roads in school (the Appian Way, the Anasazi roads in the American Southwest). We write books about roads (*On the Road, Blue Highways*). We make metaphors of roads ("take the high road," "the road to fame and fortune," "the road to hell is paved with good intentions").

But roads are also tangible creations that have been around since the invention of the wheel, if not longer. A loose consensus has it that wheels were first invented for spinning clay into plates, cups, and pots around 3500 BC. The first use of the wheel in transportation is thought to have occurred around three hundred years later.

Roads make our society and our economy possible. Roads allow cars, trucks, and buses to move from place to place, carrying goods and passengers. Those vehicles, in turn, have transformed our economics, our politics, our social interactions, our habits, our behavior, and our ways of viewing the world. They have opened once-remote areas to development. They have made life easier in many ways. They have also made it faster, more polluted, and less stable. Struggles over fuel to keep the engines running have dominated current events for decades, and, at present, concern over global climate change is causing hard reinvestigation of the effects of burning gasoline and diesel fuel to power our millions of vehicles.

But this is not a story about automobiles or trucks or petroleum. It is a story about wildlands that have been spared from the road builders, at least so far: some deliberately, some accidentally, some by default, and some as the result of perhaps the most extensive public environmental campaign in the nation's history.

So powerful, symbolically and physically, are roads and the idea of roads, that the lands that concern us here—undeveloped parts of our national forests—are defined by what they don't have: roads. They are called road-less areas. They could as well be called resortless areas, or prisonless areas, or universityless areas, but they are roadless areas, because it is roads that lead to all the rest.

Nearly 400,000 miles of roads on the 193 million acres in the country's 155 national forests and national grasslands have led to a stunning volume of destruction. Hillsides have been clear-cut, leading to landslides that have destroyed homes and wrecked spawning beds for salmon, trout, and many other aquatic species. Roads have led to the decimation of numerous pop-ulations of wildlife—the northern spotted owl and the northern Rockies grizzly bear, to name just two. Roads have made it possible for alien species to invade, gain a foothold, and spread, crowding out native species, bring-ing instability to ecosystems, and costing the economy billions of dollars. In fact, it is now estimated that this invasion of exotic species poses as serious a problem to native wildlife as habitat destruction does.

It is possible to obliterate roads (*decommission* them is how the Forest Service tends to refer to the practice) and restore landscapes, vegetation, wildlife populations, and streams, but it is expensive, and the backlog of roads needing attention is enormous. Once built, most roads remain in place for many years. Every road buries land that could be used for something else; destroys habitat for myriad creatures, if only the tiny, nearly invisible ones; and is likely to increase erosion that eventually ends up in one waterway or another.

In addition, roads have increased the risk and severity of wildfire. They have left unsightly scars that persist for decades. Finally, roads have led to the replacement of verdant, complex, ancient ecosystems with tree farms, where all the trees are the same age and the same species. The lack of diver-sity makes such areas poor habitat for many species that once thrived in the undisturbed forests and increases the forests' vulnerability to pests and disease.

In the following chapters, you will read about the Roadless Area Conservation Rule put in place at the end of the Bill Clinton administration to protect vulnerable national forest lands, and a substitute rule that the George W. Bush administration issued to replace the Clinton rule. The Bush rule invited governors to propose management schemes for the national forests in their states. We explain why the Clinton Roadless Rule was deemed necessary and how it came to be. We discuss why and how the Bush administration and its allies tried to undo it. We speak of the value of roadless areas—not just in dollars, but also for wildlife habitat, watershed protection, recreation, and the many other contributions these areas offer. We discuss the massive, unprecedented grassroots effort that pushed the Roadless Area Conservation Rule into being and kept pushing to force the inclusion of the Tongass National Forest in its purview, then rose again to defend the rule once the political tides changed. And we offer an extensive history and analysis of the legal battles concerning the two rules that raged back and forth for a half-dozen years and more—and in fact have yet to end. They may never end.

The campaign for the Roadless Rule has been the most extensive national environmental campaign yet waged in the United States, combining grassroots organizing in nearly every state; massive infusions of philanthropic support; support from hunters and anglers, religious leaders, scientists, and the outdoor recreation industry; relentless lobbying of Congress and the executive branch; and complex and extremely long-lived litigation that kept the rule in place in the face of hostile opposition.

This is what drew me to the story in the late 1990s. My organization, Earthjustice, where I've worked since 1986 as a writer and editor, was involved in protecting the nation's wildlands from the start, from well before the Roadless Rule itself came into being. At first it was very similar to a hundred other battles over the fate of public lands, but it veered into new territory when the Bush administration abandoned the legal defense of the Roadless Rule, and the private environmental organizations stepped into the breach and kept the rule alive for a half-dozen years and beyond.

I believe this is a story to be learned from and, mostly, emulated. It was, and still is, an example of how the system can work when all the pieces fall into place, with cooperation among all the elements of the environmental movement—local groups and individuals determined to protect favored spots;

national organizations that may represent local interests but also concern themselves with national policies; members of the executive branch who go into government to serve the public interest, but still need support from outside; and, finally, national organizations that concentrate on using the legal system to backstop progress achieved in the legislative arena or via federal rules and executive orders. Without these lawyers, the rest could be in vain.

As long as there are valuable trees standing on public lands, there will be someone wanting to cut them down and feed them into sawmills and pulp mills. So far, many millions of acres have been spared by the Roadless Rule and many other efforts for people here now and for those yet to come.

A note on sources: I conducted extensive interviews with the principal players in the story—Mike Dombeck, Mark Rey, Jim Lyons, Marty Hayden, Josh Reichert, Steve Kallick, Mat Jacobson, and many others. Unless otherwise noted, the quotes in the text are taken from those interviews.

Likewise, I use extensive quotes from legal briefs and motions and from published court opinions, which are cited in appendix 3. The briefs are part of the various court records available from the relevant courts. Some are available online through the courts. Most are available from Westlaw, an electronic legal archive. Some are posted on various organizations' web sites. There are vast stores of information, legal and otherwise, on the Forest Service's web site (www.roadless.fs.fed.us), and from the web sites of the Heritage Forests Campaign (www.ourforests.org), Earthjustice (www.earthjustice.org), The Wilderness Society (www.wilderness.org), and many other organizations that participated in the struggle and continue to do so.

Showdown in Cheyenne 2

IT IS A BRIGHT DAY near the end of October 2007. The stark, face-less Joseph C. Mahoney Center in Cheyenne, Wyoming, crouches across the way from the beautiful old state capitol with its golden dome gleaming in the morning sun. The wind is blowing a fierce gale, whipping autumn leaves up and down the sidewalks. Inside the courthouse, a hearing is about to get under way before the honorable Clarence Brimmer, Wyoming District Court judge.

Clarence Addison Brimmer Jr. is, in many ways, a prototypical twentieth-century westerner, determined to preserve the way of life that produced him, even in the face of vast changes. Brimmer was born in Rawlins, Wyoming, in 1922 and attended the University of Michigan for both undergraduate and law school, with a stint as an enlisted man in the Air Force in between. He was in private law practice in Rawlins for twenty-five years before serving five years as Wyoming's attorney general and one year as the U.S. attorney for Wyoming. He was appointed to the federal district court by President Gerald Ford in 1975. He was chief judge for the District of Wyoming from 1986 to 1992 and assumed senior status (which confers a lightened caseload) in 2006. Rawlins is the seat of Carbon County, named for the coal that under-lies south-central Wyoming. Brimmer's passion is raising orchids, which takes some doing in Wyoming.

Another Brimmer passion, according to people who have attended hearings in his courtroom, is a fierce antipathy to President Bill Clinton, his administration, and everything it stood for and did. Given the rural nature of Wyoming (it is one of only three states—Alaska and Montana are the others —that have just one member in the U.S. House of Representatives), much of the business that comes before the federal court concerns natural resources and the great outdoors.

In the case to be argued today, the State of Wyoming has asked the judge to declare illegal the Roadless Area Conservation Rule, which bans road building on about fifty million acres on the country's national forests. In fact, this is the second time this matter has come before Judge Brimmer. He declared this same rule illegal in 2003, but three years later another federal judge reinstated it.

Judge Brimmer walks to the bench to face a half-full courtroom, now standing upon his entrance.

At the plaintiff's table are Bob Nicholas, senior assistant attorney general of Wyoming, who will argue for the state. He is accompanied by the newly appointed attorney general, Bruce Salzburg, and a young attorney named Tara Nelson.

At the defendants' table are Jim Angell and Andrew Hartsig of the non-profit law firm Earthjustice. They represent the Wyoming Outdoor Council, The Wilderness Society, the Sierra Club, the Biodiversity Conservation Alliance, the Pacific Rivers Council, the Natural Resources Defense Council, Defenders of Wildlife, and the National Audubon Society. These groups have intervened in the case on the side of the federal government.

The original case was filed by the State of Wyoming—the plaintiff—against the federal government—the defendant. Under federal court rules, interested parties may petition to intervene in a case to protect their own interests and bolster one side's or the other's arguments. Potential intervenors must demonstrate that they have a legitimate interest in the case, which usually means that they will be "injured" in some way if the case doesn't come out the way they want it to. The alleged injury to the environmental-group intervenors in this case involves the fact that recreational opportunities of various kinds would be impaired by the destruction of roadless areas. Potential intervenors also must be able to argue that their interests will not be adequately represented by the existing parties or they are uniquely suited to add vital information and reasoning to help the court reach a correct decision.

Sometimes intervention is at the discretion of the judge, sometimes it's automatic. In the Roadless Rule case, the environmental groups have argued that their members use roadless areas for hiking, hunting, fishing, wildlife viewing, camping, or other purposes. They have also suggested that the defendant—the U.S. Department of Agriculture (USDA) Forest Service—might not mount a stout defense of the Roadless Rule. Once granted intervention, the intervenors are full parties to the case with rights to participate in briefing, in oral argument, in discovery (the questioning of representatives of the opposing parties), in settlement negotiations, and in other activities associated with the litigation.

Also at the defendants' table are Barclay Samford from the U.S. Department of Justice in Washington, DC (he answers to Clay), and Nick Vassallo, an assistant U.S. attorney for the District of Wyoming. The Justice Department officials are in a rather ambiguous position. The federal government, in this case the USDA Forest Service, represented by the Department of Justice, is no fan of the Roadless Rule. In the earlier round of litigation in this same court, it lost and later declined to appeal Judge Brimmer's injunction. Clay Samford will surprise many in the audience, later in the hearing.

In the gallery are an Associated Press reporter and representatives from both supporters and opponents of the rule, many of whom have submitted friend-of-the-court (amicus curiae) briefs with their particular slant on the controversy. These include lawyers representing the Blue Ribbon Coalition, which works to keep public lands open to Jeeps, dirt bikes, dune buggies, snowmobiles, and other off-road vehicles, and an attorney from the Colorado Mining Association. Friends of the court need permission to submit briefs, which is at the discretion of the court and usually granted. They are not parties to a case. They often present narrow interests to make certain that one particular line of argument gets a full airing. Organizations that petition for intervenor status and are turned down often file amicus briefs instead.

The judge sits down and, in a deep but rather faint voice, says, "Please be seated."

Note: Unless otherwise noted, all of the quotes that follow are taken directly from the *Transcript of Motion Proceedings Before the Honorable Clarence A. Brimmer*, U.S. District Court, Case No. 07-CV-017-B.

The Roadless Area Conservation Rule that will be argued over this day was written by officials of the Clinton administration after several years of debate, discussion, and public hearings. It forbids logging, mining, and road construction on *inventoried roadless areas* (IRAS) on the national forests, which are, generally, unroaded areas of at least five thousand acres not already protected as wilderness. Exceptions are included for roads built for fire and pest control. As of early 2001, when the rule was made official, there were approximately 58.5 million acres of such roadless areas, mainly in the West and in Alaska, with pockets scattered around the rest of the country. The final rule was challenged in nine separate lawsuits in various parts of the country, filed by states, as in the Wyoming litigation, and also by timber companies, counties, off-road-vehicle enthusiasts, and an Indian tribe. These parties objected to a national rule, arguing that forest management decisions are best left to people and agencies located close to each forest.

The first two cases of the nine were filed in Idaho in early 2001. There, Judge Edward Lodge found the rule illegal and issued a nationwide preliminary injunction. He argued that the Forest Service did not allow enough public participation in the rule's creation and that the agency had not considered a wide enough range of alternatives (for example, no roads, a few roads, certain kinds of roads, and so on). Judge Lodge's injunction was overturned by the Ninth Circuit Court of Appeals, although it was the environmental intervenors who filed the appeal, not the federal government.

Judge Brimmer then struck down the rule in 2003 for similar reasons, plus an alleged violation of the Wilderness Act. Wyoming District Court is in the Tenth Circuit, so the Ninth Circuit reversal of Judge Lodge did not apply to the case in Judge Brimmer's court. The Forest Service, which had offered a fairly vigorous defense of the rule before Judge Brimmer, did not file an appeal of the decision this time either. The environmental intervenors did, but the Tenth Circuit did not act on the appeal before the Bush administration replaced the rule with a new one of its own. Thereupon, the Tenth Circuit, at the urging of the State of Wyoming, dismissed the appeal and, at the urging of an Earthjustice attorney, vacated Judge Brimmer's injunction. We'll untangle this a bit further on. Let's say it's a proper briar patch and leave it at that for now.

In September 2006, the Clinton Roadless Rule had been resurrected by Magistrate Judge Elizabeth Laporte in California, who struck down the Bush replacement rule. The Bush rule invited governors to submit petitions suggesting how the forests in their states should be managed. Now, Wyoming has returned to Judge Brimmer's court, hoping to persuade him to issue another injunction, in effect, to supersede Judge Laporte's injunction.

Judge Brimmer sets the ground rules: "I hate like the dickens to set times for you because I think that's often unfair. The main thing is that everybody ought to get a chance to say his piece and I know that some of you could talk all day on these issues, but we can't do that. . . . I've got until four o'clock this afternoon scheduled for this so you can all use that time."

It is now 10 a.m. Hearings like this one rarely last more than an hour, but Judge Brimmer is famous for marathon hearings. He often lets everyone—plaintiffs, defendants, intervenors, friends of the court—speak their piece.

Before calling the first attorney, the judge says that he knows there will be many issues discussed and argued over today, but

> *studying this thing last night, I still have really one principal problem, and that is the Magistrate in San Francisco in effect reversed me, and I've never been reversed by a Magistrate before. But her reasoning, I thought, was peculiar. How in the world, when this Court had held that the roadless rule adopted in violence to the environmental laws, principally* NEPA *[the National Environmental Policy Act] and the Wilderness Act, and therefore, it was unconstitutional—I don't quite understand her reasoning as to when she held that the Bush Wilderness Act, or Roadless Act, was unconstitutional, she said that automatically revived the Clinton roadless rule. If any of you can tell me how that works, I would sure like to know it, because I don't think that could possibly be what the law is. That's one of the things I hope that somebody will touch on in the course of the arguments today.*

Several will try.

A magistrate is a judge appointed by a federal court, not by the president. It isn't a lifetime appointment, and it isn't confirmed by the Senate. Magistrates are often appointed to limited terms to ease the workload for overworked judges. Generally, magistrates' rulings are reviewed by tenured judges (named Article III judges for the section of the Constitution that authorizes their appointment), but in the cases filed in California, the plaintiff states, the environmental organizations, and the federal defendants agreed that Judge Laporte's ruling would stand as the ruling of the district court and any appeal of her ruling or rulings would go directly to the Ninth Circuit Court of Appeals.

Wyoming's advocate, Bob Nicholas, speaks first. He is tall and the only attorney not wearing basic black, favoring instead a tan suit. His goal is to convince Judge Brimmer to repeat his earlier declaration that the Clinton Roadless Rule is illegal in Wyoming and all other states. He launches into his argument, which is virtually identical to the argument the state made in its original attack on the rule, which began in the spring of 2001. The rule was illegal then, he says, as Judge Brimmer correctly found, and since almost nothing has changed, it's illegal now. We need an injunction against the rule that covers the whole country just like the injunction that Judge Brimmer issued in 2003, he says. Some of the parties to this proceeding—the Justice Department and some of the state's *amici curiae*—have politely suggested that if Judge Brimmer feels he must enjoin the Clinton rule again, he should limit the injunction to the national forests in Wyoming.

The judge at this point interrupts to say, "I don't really feel that I have much authority that goes beyond the state boundaries, but if you take the position that the Clinton roadless rule violated our national environmental laws, then you say, therefore, it doesn't apply in Wyoming, and of course the same ruling is, therefore, it doesn't apply anywhere else either."

Nicholas misses no chance to invoke Bill Clinton's name, evidently aware of the disdain the judge holds for the former president, who currently aspires to become the first First Gentleman. He makes repeated assertions that Clinton obviously wanted to get the Roadless Rule in place before the end of his term, no matter what, and cut many corners in order to do it.

Nicholas complains about the amount of time the Forest Service allowed for public comment on the Clinton rule prior to its adoption. Wyoming had asked the agency to extend the deadline for letters and emails, and the agency had refused. In fact, the fifty-nine days the agency provided for comment was 50 percent longer than required by law.

Nicholas suggests that the whole environmental review process was a sham—that the final decision was a foregone conclusion and that all the hearings and comments were simply for show. Judge Brimmer nods, evidently sharing this view. Nicholas repeats another argument that Judge Brimmer seems to agree with: that protecting roadless areas is the same as declaring them wilderness areas, and only Congress has the legal authority to create wilderness areas. The attorney complains that the Forest Service refused to accept applications from Wyoming and other states to become "cooperating agencies." We'll discuss these arguments at length later on.

Nicholas, however, saves most of his scorn for Judge Laporte and her September 2006 ruling, even though what she ruled—that the Bush Roadless

Rule is illegal—is not on the agenda here today, is not before Judge Brimmer at all.

This tension between judges Brimmer and Laporte brings on some perorations from Bob Nicholas and Clay Samford on *comity*. Comity generally means civility or courtesy, but in the legal community it means that a judge in one district ought to go out of his or her way to avoid stepping on the toes of a judge in another district. In this case, Nicholas argues that it is Judge Laporte who has violated the "general principles of comity," since she should have respected Judge Brimmer's 2003 injunction even though it had been dismissed by the court of appeals. Mat Jacobson of the Heritage Forests Campaign, who has worked in these trenches for eight years, whispers, "Is this a comity of errors?"

Nicholas continues his litany of criticisms, arguing that the range of alternatives the Forest Service considered was too limited and saying that squabbling over roadless areas has stopped the Forest Service from fighting insect infestations in roadless areas, areas now prone to devastating wildfire. He suggests that the maps the Forest Service provided were useless, outdated, and inaccurate. Judge Brimmer weighs in, noting that back when he was in private practice representing farmers, ranchers, and mining companies, the Forest Service had marvelous maps and aerial photographs. He comes close to suggesting that the agency deliberately withheld good maps from the public during the Roadless Rule hearing process: "They could have had accurate maps and published them and put them out, but they didn't do it."

Nicholas renews his plea for a nationwide injunction and takes his seat, saying that he'll no doubt need to offer rebuttals later in the day to arguments yet to be made. Judge Brimmer calls a five-minute recess.

Next up is Clay Samford from the Department of Justice, a trim, close-cropped fellow who has been representing the Forest Service in much of the roadless litigation throughout the country. In papers filed prior to the hearing, the government has taken the position that any injunction the judge feels compelled to issue should be limited to the State of Wyoming. "The posture of this case is unique," he begins, saying that the 2001 rule is no longer the policy of the Forest Service. The agency favors the Bush 2005 rule, which has been declared illegal by Judge Laporte. The Justice Department, he reports, has appealed Judge Laporte's injunction and hopes to prevail. Then he stuns some of the observers by stating: "We believe that the roadless rule as promulgated in 2000 complied with all applicable laws and regulations."

This is a surprise because the government had offered something less than a half hearted defense of the rule in the Idaho court over six years ago and had declined to appeal adverse rulings both there and, later, in Judge Brimmer's case. Greg Shafer of Arch Coal, a large mining corporation, sitting in the audience this day, is quite flabbergasted, plainly taken by surprise.

Armchair analysts suggest at least two rationales for the federal government's taking this position this time around. One is that the government, after all, took a similar position in written briefs in the original Wyoming litigation, even though it refused to defend the rule once Judge Lodge and Judge Brimmer found against it. A second theory has it that the government understands that if the Roadless Rule, which involved a more extensive public process than any comparable federal rule in history, doesn't comply with the public-participation requirements of federal law, nothing ever will. The government does not believe the 2001 Roadless Rule is the best way to manage the forests, Samford tells the judge, but it does believe the rule was legally adopted, and an injunction would be inappropriate.

Instead, Samford suggests that if Judge Brimmer finds the 2001 rule legal or if he feels compelled to find it illegal or invalid, he could remand it to the Forest Service for revision without issuing any injunction. Or if the judge feels he must issue an injunction, the federal government hopes he will limit it to Wyoming.

There's some considerable legal logic behind this suggestion. Wyoming is the only plaintiff in this case, and the harm it claims the Clinton rule would cause would therefore be limited to Wyoming. Extending the relief beyond the state's boundaries would please some of the *amici*—the Blue Ribbon Coalition, the Colorado Mining Association, and others that have members in many states—but they're not parties to the case, at least not yet.

Samford then rebuts most of the arguments put forward by Wyoming's lawyer. The public had ample opportunity to participate in the development of the rule, he says, and the range of alternatives was more than adequate; the states had plenty of chances to speak their piece, and they did so. The government, in short, has the legal authority to do what it did.

Samford adds a point that loomed large in the original conception and development of the rule. There are hundreds of thousands of miles of abandoned roads in the national forests that are falling into streams, wrecking habitat for fish and other wild creatures, and occasionally triggering land-slides that destroy homes. The Forest Service estimates that it would take around $10 billion to fix this problem, money the agency doesn't have and has little prospect of getting. "So it seemed to defy common sense for the agency to be considering building even more roads in areas previously unroaded when we had this backlog of dealing with existing roads," Samford states.

He then takes on the Wilderness Act argument, pointing out some of the activities (grazing, off-road vehicle use, placing of structures, and oil and gas operations, among others) that are permitted in roadless areas but forbidden in wilderness areas.

Finally, he points out that the Forest Service spends much money and effort to fight insects and thin forests to reduce their vulnerability to fire, money that will be spent on projects close to towns and houses, not in remote roadless areas, no matter which rule eventually survives. If any. The fire argument, he repeats, has no merit.

It is approaching noon. Jim Angell walks to the lectern. Angell is about the same age as the other attorneys, forty-something, at a guess. He's tall and wears thick-rimmed glasses, hair cut short. He represents the environmental groups that have joined the case on the side of the Forest Service. He has been involved in this case since it was filed in early 2001. His objective is to persuade Judge Brimmer that the 2001 Clinton Roadless Rule is completely legal, was legally adopted, is good public policy, and should be retained in force. His is a very steep hill to climb.

Angell starts off with a little oratory:

> *Your Honor, we stand here in a court of law, not within the halls of a leg-islature, so the questions for us here are not whether the roadless rule is a good policy, whether a different policy might be a better idea. . . . We have an altogether more humble task in front of us, which we are to undertake with all due humility, and that's just to figure out whether what was done was legal. . . . Rhetoric about the political motivations of an agency, or even worse yet, the political motivations of a sister court, should not have any purchase power in the court today. So I'm going to focus on the law and the record, and I will try to keep my rhetoric to a minimum.*

"That sounds fine to me," Judge Brimmer replies.

Angell echoes the arguments put forward by Clay Samford. The hearing process was perfectly legal and in line with federal regulations. Comment periods were ample. Maps may have been imperfect, but there is no legal requirement that maps be provided at all.

Judge Brimmer interrupts: "If I were an old Wyoming rancher...."

"Your honor, there is no Wyoming rancher before this court."

Angell soldiers on: "It is completely discretionary whether the government makes states or other entities cooperating agencies." This was another of Wyoming's complaints.

The National Environmental Policy Act gives federal agencies the authority to sign up cooperating agencies (states, cities, tribes) to help them write environmental impact studies when that would make for a more effective process. In this case, the lead agency, the Forest Service, declined to invite in any cooperating agencies because of the scope of the rule. Invite one state, you'd have to invite thirty or forty. Invite one tribe, and you'd have to invite dozens more. Same with cities. George Frampton, chairman of the Council on Environmental Quality, explained this to a congressional committee in 2000, as the hearing process for the Roadless Rule was getting going:

> This is one of the circumstances in which we believe that a "cooperating agency" designation in the strict sense of the word is not feasible or appropriate; indeed, we know of no example of a non-federal cooperating agency for an EIS [environmental impact statement] of national scope. There are potentially hundreds of cooperating agencies, given the number of states, counties, and tribal governments in the country. From a management perspective, allocating work assignments among these widespread agencies is not feasible or practical.

The states, Wyoming in particular, were very unhappy with this decision and have brought it up repeatedly in the litigation, suggesting that the Forest Service under Clinton had deliberately excluded them from the planning for roadless areas.

Brimmer again: "Don't you really think that the agency, because the president had told them to pass this rule, had prejudged the case, made up their minds, and were going to do that regardless of what anybody said?"

"There's nothing in the record to support that, your honor," Angell says. "Nothing to indicate bad faith. There is no question President Clinton wanted to get the rule through by the end of his term, your honor. There's no law against that. It's not unusual; it's normal. All presidents do it."

It's twelve-thirty. The judge halts proceedings for lunch. The hearing resumes at one-thirty with Angell again at the lectern. He reinforces Clay Samford's argument about fire, pointing out that there are forty pages of fire analysis in the environmental impact statement concerning the original rule and that the Forest Service concentrates its fire-suppression efforts near homes and other buildings, not in the backcountry.

"I presume that's right," says the judge. "Well, I presume that's right because I've got the idea that in a roadless area they are just going to let it burn."

Angell then takes on the argument that only Congress may create wilderness areas. He rattles off short sections of three different laws. The Forest Service's Organic Act (1897), the law that brought the agency into being a century ago, says that the agriculture secretary, who oversees the Forest Service, may issue rules to protect the reserves—"to protect the forests thereon from destruction." The Multiple-Use Sustained-Yield Act, which became law in 1960, says that "the establishment and maintenance of areas of wilderness are consistent with the purposes and provisions of this Act." And the Wilderness Act, adopted in 1964, says "nothing in this Act shall be deemed to be in interference with the purposes for which national forests are established as set forth in" the two laws in question. Judge Brimmer does not look convinced.

The matter of Magistrate Judge Elizabeth Laporte resurfaces. The judge says, "You know, a Magistrate is just a federal JP [justice of the peace], and I will be darned if I think that she can pass a rule that I have to obey. I'm willing to obey the Court of Appeals and the supremes, but not a Magistrate."

Angell repeats the argument that Judge Laporte's authority is the same as any Article III judge's and points out that Judge Brimmer's injunction has been vacated, and Judge Laporte is simply following the mandate of the Ninth Circuit. He takes his seat.

Next, Judge Brimmer asks if any of the *amici's* lawyers would like to speak. They have been watching and listening intently from the gallery.

First is Paul Turcke, another slim, forty-something male with close-cropped hair, in a dark suit. He represents the Blue Ribbon Coalition, which he says has been involved in all the roadless lawsuits. He then proceeds to make a rather startling assertion that Judge Laporte didn't mean what she said. Or didn't say what she meant, it wasn't altogether clear. "If Judge Laporte said that 'I'm staking out my ground and nobody else in the world, Judge Brimmer or anyone else, can declare unlawful a rule that I'm not even passing judgment on,' then I don't think that's what she really meant. And you know, judges are human and they sometimes say things that they will ultimately regret, just like all of us. And if, in fact, that's what she said, I think she was just in fact flat wrong."

Turcke then encourages Judge Brimmer to take a cue from his own previous injunction, which had been vacated by order of the Tenth Circuit Court of Appeals: "A vacated decision, particularly one that comes from outside the controlling circuit, can be given as much persuasive value as the Court deems it entitled to," he says, suggesting that Judge Laporte should have paid deference to Judge Brimmer's previous injunction, even though it had been vacated by the Tenth Circuit.

Next comes Harriet Hageman, dressed in electric blue. She represented Wyoming in the early rounds of this litigation and is clearly at ease with Judge Brimmer. "Good afternoon, Judge," she says, and he smiles his welcome. She now represents the Blue Ribbon Coalition along with Paul Turcke.

She zeroes in on the Idaho case, which was decided before Judge Brimmer found the 2001 rule illegal. In that case, Judge Edward Lodge in Boise had found the rule illegal for some of the same reasons Judge Brimmer cited. Judge Lodge's injunction was appealed to the Ninth Circuit Court of Appeals in San Francisco, and the injunction was thrown out. The appellate court's ruling suggested that it thought the rule itself was legal, which provided the backdrop to Judge Laporte's later injunction and reinstatement order.

Ms. Hageman demurs. "The Ninth Circuit did not look into the merits of the roadless rule at any time. It never has. [In fact, it did, as will be discussed later.] . . . . There's only one court that's looked at . . . the roadless rule and, Judge, that's you. That's it." She insists that the aim of the rule and its proponents is "to stop everything in these areas." These are wilderness areas, she insists, no matter what others may claim. "We don't have to check our common sense at the courthouse door when we come into court," she says, a phrase she repeats a few minutes later. She then blames the Roadless Rule for the wildfires that have scorched the West in recent years.

Next to speak is Timothy Odil from the Colorado Mining Association, who complains that Judge Brimmer's magistrate refused to let his organization intervene in the case, though it has submitted a friend-of-the-court brief. "You may intervene," the judge says. "This is like a town meeting." Jim Angell of Earthjustice winces. This may strengthen the argument put forward by some that any injunction should be nationwide, since the association has members in many states, not just Wyoming. As full parties to the case, the association can argue that its interests—and the harm the Clinton rule allegedly does to them—extend well beyond the state's boundary.

Odil's concern is that the Roadless Rule restricts the ability of his members to mine: "Two hundred million tons of coal would be lost to Arch Coal alone" if the Clinton rule is sustained, he says. Coal has been getting a great deal of bad press lately for its leading role in global warming, and big new coal plant proposals have just been shelved in Florida, Washington, and Nebraska, so the market for coal may be getting a little shaky, but that's another story.

The principal attorneys now take turns wrapping up. Clay Samford again argues against an injunction since, if there are contradictory injunctions in force (one from Judge Laporte, one from Judge Brimmer), the "Forest Service will be forced with the very real choice of deciding which court they want to go and defend contempt charges in." What he means is this: Suppose you are in charge of a national forest. Almost any national forest. Weyerhaeuser or Boise Cascade or Louisiana Pacific or another company applies for permission to log a roadless area in your forest. If you refuse, citing Judge Laporte's injunction, you are defying Judge Brimmer's injunction, assuming he issues a broad-brush injunction. Conversely, if you approve the timber sale, you're defying Judge Laporte's injunction, so you're in contempt of one court or the other. Not a pretty circumstance to contemplate. Clay Samford's appeal hangs quietly in the air.

Jim Angell repeats that this is a court of law. All we're here to decide is whether a law has been broken, not whether the Roadless Rule is a policy that people, states, or agencies like. "The issue here is whether the rule was adopted legally, not whether it should be something different."

Bob Nicholas renews his request for an immediate nationwide injunction against the 2001 rule.

With that, Judge Brimmer announces that he has a lot of reading to do (there must be close to fifty briefs filed in this case so far, and ten volumes of the administrative record), so we're not to expect a decision too soon. The hearing ends a little after four o'clock.

The decision gestates for nine and a half months. On August 12, 2008, as the Olympics and the conflict in the former Soviet republic of Georgia monopolize the front pages, the judge issues a 104-page decision, which includes a nationwide injunction against the Roadless Rule.

It closely parallels the injunction he issued in 2003, finding that the 2001 rule violates both the National Environmental Policy Act and the Wilderness Act.

Specifically, Judge Brimmer rules, "The Court, as it did in [the previous case], finds that: (1) the Forest Service's decision not to extend the scoping comment period was arbitrary and capricious; (2) the Forest Service's denial of cooperating agency status without explanation was arbitrary and capricious; (3) the Forest Service's failure to rigorously explore and objectively evaluate all reasonable alternatives was contrary to law; (4) the Forest Service's conclusion that its cumulative impacts analysis in the Roadless Rule Final EIS satisfied NEPA duties was a clear error in judgment; and (5) the Forest Service's decision not to issue a supplemental EIS was arbitrary, capricious, and contrary to law." (*Order Granting Plaintiff's Motion for Declaratory Judgment and Injunctive Relief,* U.S. District Court, Case No. 07-CV-017-B)

He adds a zinger or two: The whole affair, he writes, "was the result of political posturing for an outgoing president."

"The Court is disturbed, and frankly shocked," he adds, "at the fact that a Magistrate Judge essentially re-instituted a policy that was not properly before that Court, and especially in light of the fact that an Article III judge [himself] had already ruled that the re-instituted policy was promulgated in violation of law."

Jim Angell of Earthjustice files an official notice of intent to appeal the decision with the Tenth Circuit the following day.

The Road to   3
Roadlessness

THE FIRST STEPS taken nationally to preserve fast-disappearing forests came in 1891, when President Benjamin Harrison set aside 13 million acres of forest reserves. In 1905, Teddy Roosevelt added 132 million acres more, renamed them national forests, and created the Forest Service to manage them. Eventually the national forest system grew to 192 million acres. A little over 35 million of those acres have been protected forever (if anything is forever) as wilderness, off-limits to all motorized activity. Well over half the national forest acreage has been logged or mined, sometimes both. As of the late 1990s, there were a carefully measured 58.5 million acres of official unprotected roadless areas, known as *inventoried roadless areas* (IRAS), on national forests across the country, with a heavy concentration in the West, especially in Alaska and Idaho.

The fate of those road-free acres has been the subject of one of the major environmental battles of the early years of the twenty-first century.

The national forests are managed by the Forest Service, an agency of the Department of Agriculture. Many attempts have been made over the years by politicians and bureaucrats, including Interior Secretary Stewart Udall, who served throughout the Kennedy and Johnson administrations, to move the agency into the Department of the Interior, where the other federal land-managing agencies (National Park Service, Bureau of Land Management,

Fish and Wildlife Service) are found, but the timber industry, among others, prefers to keep the tree managers to the side where it can keep an eye on them and continue to ensure that forests are first and foremost a crop to be harvested (some conservation groups prefer to keep the Forest Service out of the Interior Department as well, since the agencies are occasionally at odds. If the Forest Service were in the Interior Department it might be more difficult to stop it from carrying out bad practices, or so the argument goes). In fact, as this is being written, in the spring of 2008, yet another proposal by congressional Republicans to move the Forest Service into the Department of the Interior has been floated and is stirring some interest.

The situation of the Forest Service in the Department of Agriculture led, particularly since World War II, to the forests' being managed primarily for timber production at the expense of the other values—recreation, habitat, watershed protection—that the forests were set aside to protect. Conservationists have been battling to tip the emphasis away from logging for years. The Sierra Club, for one example, along with the John Muir Project and other organizations, has taken the position that there should be no commercial logging at all on the national forests—a *zero-cut* policy. This policy was established in 1996 after renegade Sierra Club members failed to sway the board of directors and so proposed a zero-cut ballot initiative that was passed by the membership by a two-to-one margin.

Other conservationists support what is often referred to as *sustained-yield* logging. Under that approach, foresters calculate how much volume of wood is added to a stand of trees in a year, as trees grow larger and new ones sprout, and limit the volume of wood cut and removed from the forest to that amount. This is a praiseworthy objective, but there's a problem. In old-growth forests, which have reached what's known as successional *climax*, there is little or no net gain in wood volume from year to year. Timber company people call these *overmature* or *moribund* forests and argue that they need to be cut to stimulate new growth.

There are many other issues as well; volume is but one consideration. The impact of logging depends also on the manner in which it is carried out. The timber industry prefers to concentrate on the biggest, oldest stands of trees, which are the most valuable, both in the amount of wood each tree provides, and in the quality of the wood—oldest is densest and has the fewest knots. Industry often prefers to engage in *clear-cutting*, which is comparable to sending a combine through a field of wheat, leveling everything in its path, then replanting with fast-growing species that can be harvested again in a few decades. This not only maximizes profits for the companies, but also maximizes damage to all the other forest values—wildlife habitat; human water supplies; and places to hunt, fish, camp, and hike.

What makes the logging (and mining, and many other activities) possible is roads. There have been experiments in removing cut trees from the woods by tying them to hot-air balloons or helicopters and lifting them straight up. It works as intended but is too expensive to be widely practical, and the felling of the trees still causes damage on the ground. There also have been experiments with vehicles called *forwarders*, which have huge rubber tires and can navigate through a forest like a Humvee, cutting trees and trampling vegetation. Conventional logging, however, where trees are felled and loaded onto log trucks, requires roads.

The interstate highway system comprises about forty thousand miles of roads (including three interstates on the island of Oahu, Hawaii, which is intriguing to contemplate). The national forests are crisscrossed by more than ten times that many miles of roads, moving David G. Havlick, in the 2002 book *No Place Distant*, to write, "The U.S. Forest Service is, far and away, the top road building agency in American history" (31).

A large fraction of the Forest Service roads, unfortunately, are unpaved and in disrepair, having served their primary purpose and been abandoned. The Forest Service classifies its roads as either *system* or *nonsystem* roads; abandoned roads are often referred to as *temporary* roads. In general, the system roads were built to serve some continuing purpose, while nonsystem roads were one-time projects, often built to provide access to a timber sale. Once the timber has been logged, the roads are often abandoned and perhaps used occasionally for recreation of one sort or another. The nonsystem roads tend to be maintained far less carefully than system roads—if they're maintained at all. In addition, there are what are often called *ghost roads* created by the passage of vehicles, usually recreational four-wheelers like Jeeps. The Forest Service estimates that there are on the order of sixty thousand miles of ghost roads on the national forests. The agency does not know how many miles of temporary roads there are. At least 80 percent of the roads on the forests are in need of work, either maintenance or decommissioning.

As of late 2004, the Forest Service estimated that it would take $10 billion to either repair or retire those roads; the agency's total road budget for one year then was $200 million. At that rate, it would take the agency fifty years to take care of its road-maintenance backlog, if it never built a mile of new road. But that simple calculation is woefully short of the mark—for every year that a road goes unmaintained, it deteriorates further, and the cost of fixing it climbs. Mike Dombeck, the Forest Service chief in the late 1990s, argued in an interview that this gigantic backlog should be considered a liability on the Forest Service's balance sheet and that it makes no sense to increase the liability by building more roads.

In 1964, after a decade-long campaign led by Howard Zahniser of The Wilderness Society, David Brower of the Sierra Club, and Representative John P. Saylor, a Republican from Ohio, Congress passed the Wilderness Act. The idea was to provide a way to identify which lands were most appropriate to set aside, inviolate, forever: "Lands," Zahniser quipped, "where the hand of man has never set foot," according to his son, Ed Zahniser, in an email to the author. Nearly all these lands would be areas already owned and operated by the federal government; most would be on national forests. For this reason the Forest Service steadfastly opposed the legislation until the last minute— even though that agency, under the prodding of Aldo Leopold and Robert Marshall, had protected a fair amount of wilderness on its own since the 1930s, calling the areas, variously, *wilderness areas, primitive areas, natural areas,* or *experimental* forests or grasslands. The legal authority for the creation of these areas is codified in the Forest Service's Organic Act (1897), the law that created the agency and gives it the power and authority, not to mention the duty, to protect its lands.

The Wilderness Act of 1964 immediately set aside 9.1 million acres of national forest land. The law gave Congress the power to set aside more unspoiled areas, such areas described as being at least five thousand acres in size and without roads. Congress directed the Forest Service to survey its lands to see what was there and which areas should be added to the National Wilderness Preservation System.

The result was RARE—the Roadless Area Review and Evaluation of 1972. It identified 12.3 million acres the Forest Service thought Congress might want to protect. When people from The Wilderness Society and other groups looked at the fine print, however, they were horrified. Millions of acres they considered prime candidates for protection had been omitted. The Wyoming Outdoor Council, represented by the Natural Resources Defense Council, filed suit under the recently enacted National Environmental Policy Act (1969) to force the agency to prepare environmental impact studies before allowing logging in roadless areas as defined by Forest Service criteria. District Judge Ewing T. Kerr in Wyoming ruled against the plaintiffs but was reversed by the Tenth Circuit Court of Appeals, which found that the Forest Service had failed to conduct required environmental studies.

The conservation groups also insisted that another inventory be conducted, and eventually the Forest Service acquiesced and undertook a second survey, known as RARE II (1979).

Meanwhile, in 1973, a lawsuit filed by the West Virginia chapter of the Izaak Walton League against the Monongahela National Forest in West Virginia argued that the very practice of clear-cutting violated the Forest Service's Organic Act. That law allowed the agency to sell, for cutting, trees that are "dead, mature, and large growth of trees... for the purpose of preserving the living and promoting the young growth on national forests." This, the lawyers argued in their brief to the court, precluded clear-cutting, which involves cutting everything, not just "dead, mature, and large... " trees. It also required that all trees to be felled be individually marked before logging, which clear-cutters do not do. The court found the argument persuasive and outlawed clear-cutting nationwide. This court ruling caused Congress to get involved. It set out to rewrite the law, producing the National Forest Management Act of 1976, which allowed the Forest Service to resume clear-cutting with certain restrictions.

RARE II recommended fifteen million acres for wilderness designation. Thirty-six million acres were dubbed *nonwilderness,* and eleven million were put into a category called *further planning.* Conservation groups were not pleased and felt that wilderness was still being shortchanged. The State of California filed suit, assisted by the Natural Resources Defense Council, and the parts of RARE II that released roadless areas for logging were declared illegal by Judge Lawrence Karlton in Sacramento, who was subsequently sustained by the Ninth Circuit. Battles raged over the fate of specific places across the country. The conservation community, determined to protect as much wildland as possible, cast about for tools to stop the Forest Service from committing too much forestland to logging.

There was little relief during Ronald Reagan's presidency (1981–89). Reagan's Interior Secretary, James Watt, was an outspoken enemy of wilderness, and he had considerable influence over Forest Service policies as well, even though he had no direct authority over the agency. The secretary of agriculture at the time was John R. Block, a West Point graduate who had been a successful farmer in Illinois and was willing to leave forest issues to others. During Block's tenure, Max Peterson was appointed chief of the Forest Service. A civil engineer, Peterson was the first nonforester to hold the position. Logging and road building, which had declined considerably since a peak in 1973, increased rapidly. An acceleration in the rate of logging inevitably leads to an acceleration of road construction.

Ironically, however, there was a considerable spurt in the designation of wilderness areas during the Reagan years: 229 new wilderness areas totaling just over ten million acres were created outside Alaska, and another 14 wildernesses comprising more than five million acres were set aside in Alaska.

Under Peterson, roads continued to snake their way across the forests as trucks hauled fallen trees to lumber and pulp mills. The harvest of logs from the national forests crept to an all-time high of close to thirteen billion board feet in 1987, a figure that was clearly not supportable in the long run. Recently, that is since 2000, the volume has fluctuated from just over to just under two billion board feet—a board foot being a piece of lumber a foot square and an inch thick. An average, medium-sized, wooden home takes about ten thousand board feet to build.

Having failed to rein in overcutting (and overroading) via the RARE process, in the mid-1990s lobbyists for the Sierra Club, The Wilderness Society, Earthjustice, and other groups came up with a new tactic—going after the Forest Service's road budget. If the agency had no money to build roads, they reasoned, the forests would be automatically protected, and it sounded as if the White House might be sympathetic to that ultimate goal, if not this particular tactic. Many timber sales across the country were costing the government far more than they brought in, and many members of Congress were losing patience with the Forest Service and its stewardship of the public's forestlands.

This was the era of Senator William Proxmire, a Wisconsin Democrat who succeeded Joseph McCarthy in the Senate. Proxmire's passion was rooting out waste in federal spending. Once a month, from 1975 to 1986, Proxmire would issue a "Golden Fleece Award" to honor an especially onerous example of government waste, whether it be a government grant for a silly research study, an overpriced piece of equipment for the military, or an outrageous junket for a member of the executive branch. An award issued in March 1984 cited a Forest Service expenditure of $40 million on four helicopters and a blimp, to see if those vehicles might be useful for transporting logs. The June 1986 award, according to a compilation by Taxpayers for Common Sense, went to the Forest Service "for appropriating and spending $51 million preparing for Alaskan timber sales which lost on average 83 cents on the dollar." These numbers remain typical.

In the House of Representatives, forest reformers found champions in Democrat Joe Kennedy of Massachusetts and Republican John Porter of Illinois. The first effort put forward in the House, in 1996, would have eliminated the $42 million road-construction budget and the $41 million *purchaser road credit*. This is money a timber company bids for a timber sale but can spend on road construction, reducing income to the federal treasury by that amount. Marty Hayden of Earthjustice calls it "Monopoly money." The Kennedy-Porter amendment passed the House on June 29, 1996, on a vote of 211 to 210. After a night of arm twisting by Representative Newt Gingrich, a Republican from Georgia, and his lieutenants, the amendment was reconsidered and went down on a tie vote, 211 to 211.

Marty Hayden is the chief policy expert for Earthjustice, a nonprofit environmental law firm with nine offices scattered around the country. The organization was founded in 1971 as the Sierra Club Legal Defense Fund but changed its name to Earthjustice in 1997. Hayden was trained as a fish biologist and worked as a fish technician on the Tongass National Forest in Alaska in 1979 and 1980. He then went to work for the Sierra Club as a lobbyist in Missouri in 1988; moved to Washington, DC, in 1990; and joined Earthjustice in 1995.

In 1997, a year after the Kennedy-Porter effort failed to pass the House, it returned, with Porter taking the lead. A nose count indicated that the amendment would pass on an up-or-down vote, so a compromise amendment to the amendment was proposed by Representative Norm Dicks of Washington. That amendment would have reduced the road budget by $5.6 million and restored $25 million in purchaser credits. The Dicks amendment passed the House by 211 to 209 but died on a tie vote in the Senate with Vice President Gore absent.

The White House had not failed to notice the trend. On November 14, 1997, buried deep in a statement marking the signing of the appropriations bill for the Interior Department and related agencies, published in the Federal Register, President Clinton wrote, "The Forest Service is developing a scientifically based policy for managing roadless areas in our national forests.

These last remaining wild areas are precious to millions of Americans and key to protecting clean water and abundant wildlife habitat, and providing recreation opportunities. These unspoiled places must be managed through science, not politics." Environmental forces took note of the president's roadless remark and began thinking about how they might capitalize on it.

Legislation was still possible, but it was contentious and difficult. Some argued that the executive branch might have the authority—if it had the will—to fix the problem without involving the legislative branch. There was talk of executive orders and federal rules. The forces determined to stop the ravaging of the national forests could feel the wind beginning to pick up at their backs.

The president's statement upon signing the appropriations bill in late 1997 had caught the eye of people in the Pew Charitable Trusts, which will be discussed extensively in chapter 5. Pew offered a grant to the National Audubon Society to fund forest-defense work, and Audubon hired Ken Rait.

Rait had spent seven years with the Southern Utah Wilderness Alliance and a year with the Oregon Natural Resources Council. His work in the Northwest involved rallying the public to rise to the defense of the forests, but the arguments there tended to involve technical matters arising from the Forest Service's new Northwest Forest Plan—aquatic conservation strategies and matrix lands among them—concepts that were hard to understand, harder to explain. The idea of working on a national campaign with a clean and simple goal of saving roadless areas was very appealing to Rait.

He convened a series of meetings that resulted in the creation of the Heritage Forests Campaign, a coalition of forest-defense groups. The campaign was a project of the National Audubon Society, with funding from Pew. The name was chosen after testing several variations on focus groups. They wanted to appeal to a broad public and to offend as few people as possible. *Heritage,* it turned out, was an attractive and relatively neutral word.

The key early players in the campaign were the National Audubon Society, valued for its grassroots network and a highly respected vice president named Dan Beard, who had been the head of the federal Bureau of Reclamation and had worked for years on Capitol Hill (Ken Rait reported to him); The Wilderness Society for its policy expertise; the Natural Resources Defense Council for its policy expertise and attorney Niel Lawrence; the American Lands Alliance for its forest experience, its connections with grassroots groups, and its leader, the former congressman Jim Jontz; the U.S. Public

Interest Research Group for its canvass operation and grassroots outreach; Earthjustice for its legal expertise; the National Environmental Trust for political and media expertise; The Technology Project, an early leader in electronic communications; Green Corps for its grassroots organizing expertise; and Defenders of Wildlife for its strong activist base and grassroots networks.

Meanwhile, the Forest Service was well aware of the growing unhappiness with its policies and activities and its narrow escapes in Congress. Its road budget was in serious jeopardy of being eliminated. Something must be done.

Enter Mike Dombeck. Dombeck is a PhD fisheries biologist who grew up in the Chequamegon National Forest in Wisconsin, twenty-five miles from the nearest town. He joined the Forest Service in 1978 where he stayed until 1989, when he moved to the Bureau of Land Management (BLM). He later moved into the Land and Minerals Management section of the Interior Department and then, in 1994, was appointed head of the BLM, to replace the colorful and outspoken Jim Baca. Baca had clashed with Interior Secretary Bruce Babbitt and former secretary Cecil Andrus and had been sacked, to the delight of the livestock industry and to the dismay of the environmental movement.

Dombeck had actively opposed a grazing bill sponsored by New Mexico Republican Senator Pete Domenici, which in Dombeck's words "was little more than giveaway of public resources to ranchers to block ... an increase in grazing fees." This was an early and controversial initiative mounted by Secretary Babbitt, which earned him and the administration considerable enmity among some western members of Congress. So, for three years Dombeck served as the acting head of the BLM—his nomination was submitted for confirmation but never voted on.

In 1996, Jack Ward Thomas, chief of the Forest Service, resigned. Thomas had tried to force decisive action on the roadless area problem by ordering his regional foresters either to recommend their areas for wilderness or to open them to road building and logging. Here's his journal entry from October 14, 1995, as it appears in his memoir, *The Journals of a Forest Service Chief*:

> *Nearly eighteen months ago, I sent out instructions to regional foresters*
> *either to remove contentious roadless areas (nearly all are contentious)*

from the timber base via forest plan amendment or to proceed forthwith
to enter those areas for purposes of timber management—i.e., initial
roading and logging. I felt it necessary to issue such instructions because
most Forest Service managers had, reasonably enough, shied away from
the controversy inherent in entry into roadless areas.

The regional foresters, according to Mike Dombeck, largely ignored Thomas.

Jim Lyons was under secretary of agriculture for Natural Resources and Environment at this time and, in that position, the boss of the chief forester. Lyons is a graduate of the Yale School of Forestry who had served as a staff assistant on the House Agriculture Committee before moving to the Department of Agriculture at the beginning of the Clinton administration. He had heard good things about Dombeck, both in his role as head of BLM and in his previous stint in the Forest Service. He asked Dombeck if he would consider becoming Forest Service chief to replace Thomas, who was about to retire. Dombeck agreed.

In the new job, Dombeck would need new people to help get the agency back on track. He wanted people who were willing to envision a Forest Service that would emphasize preservation over exploitation. One name that was suggested by a key ally as Dombeck cast about for a deputy was that of Jim Furnish.

Furnish was the supervisor of the Siuslaw National Forest in Oregon. On a trip there years before, he and a friend had caught (and released) sixty Umpqua cutthroat trout in Squaw Creek in two hours. By the time he took over as supervisor of the forest, the fish were gone, victims of out-of-control logging. He set out to start the long process of bringing the forest back to health. Roads were key.

Furnish launched an experimental program to "treat" several abandoned roads, in a system where ditches and culverts are removed or filled in and replaced by "water bars" that direct water away from the road surface before it can cause too much erosion. Nature will take care of the rest. This technique is quicker and far less costly than a full-scale decommissioning of the roads, which involves much heavy equipment, recontouring the roadbed, and replanting vegetation.

In 1996, a huge storm hit the Siuslaw area, causing catastrophic landslides that damaged homes and businesses, not to mention streams and habitat for salmon, steelhead, and other species. After the storm moved on,

Furnish went out to inspect the treated roads. They had held. He decided that one of his big responsibilities was to start a major restoration effort on the forest, taking the long term into account. Over the next several years, under his prodding, three-quarters of the roads on the Siuslaw disappeared, and fish and their habitat began a dramatic recovery. By the time he left the Forest Service, big-tree logging had almost entirely stopped and, as he put it in an interview, "you couldn't see the roads." Even in Oregon, where logging had been almost a religion, the restoration program was a hit. "By the 1990s," Furnish says, "the public was more interested in naturalness, water, wildlife, personal renewal, and future generations."

Elsewhere, attempts to eliminate roads and restore habitat had occasionally run into resistance from some hunters and off-highway-vehicle enthusiasts who feared losing roads they enjoyed using, but in western Oregon restoration was quite popular.

Chris Wood, a graduate of Middlebury College, had come with Dombeck from the BLM to the Forest Service to be the new chief's majordomo. Wood knew Furnish and greatly admired the work he had done on the Siuslaw National Forest. He mentioned the Siuslaw experience to Mike Dombeck. Dombeck consulted with people inside and outside the agency and got the impression that Furnish was bright, energetic, and willing to take risks. Dombeck decided to invite Furnish to come to Washington to be deputy chief for the national forests, in which position he would oversee all the regional foresters in the system. Furnish was skeptical. He knew the appointment would be controversial within the agency, because Furnish, a forest supervisor, would be leapfrogging over all the regional foresters, from whose ranks the deputies were usually chosen. But Dombeck was out to shake up the agency, and he thought Furnish was the man to do it. Furnish agreed.

Mike Dombeck was well aware of how close the Forest Service had come to losing its road budget, and he began to think about ways to deal with the problem. As he tells it, following a staff meeting he was chatting with Greg Freizer, assistant to Agriculture Secretary Dan Glickman. Former chief Jack Ward Thomas, Dombeck related, had famously described the Forest Service as a "rudderless ship with a muddled mission." Dombeck took a different view. He blamed Congress for putting the agency into gridlock, too whipsawed to take positions on important issues. "We were being mealy-mouthed. All defensive," Dombeck said. "We needed to come up with something positive."

Glickman, who had been listening quietly, said, "OK, develop a plan."

"Oh dear, what have I done?" Dombeck quietly asked himself. The problem, as he saw it, was severalfold. First, the agency tried to please everybody. Western legislators, including Senator Larry Craig of Idaho and Representative Bob Smith of Oregon, kept introducing bills aimed at forcing the Forest Service to increase logging dramatically at the expense of environmental protection. The Forest Service would respond by saying that it agreed with the goal of the legislation but had trouble with the details. Second, there was this gigantic backlog of road maintenance that the agency couldn't begin to keep up with. "There was an $8 billion backlog of undone maintenance, which I always referred to as a taxpayer liability," Dombeck said in an interview. He also said that "the Republicans on the Hill didn't like that term, but that's what it is. I was CEO and I had a liability of $8 billion [by 2008, the number had risen above $10 billion]. Who would invest in more roads and just increase his liability?" At the same time the agency would assure environmental groups that it was a staunch protector of the forests.

Finally, the arguments over money for building roads had become inextricably tangled with arguments over roadless areas. Dombeck felt that they must be separated if there was any hope of solving either. He scratched his head. Then he had a truly revolutionary thought. "I wonder if I can simply declare a moratorium on road building," he asked himself. He asked the agency's lawyers, who said they thought he could. He knew there would be hell to pay, but thought it worth the effort. But first, he had to convince his colleagues. If we can pull this off, he told himself, it will prove that the Forest Service can once again lead and not simply sit back and wait to get pushed around by politicians. A key to the success of such an effort would be to shift the loyalties of the men and women who work for the agency from the institution to the land itself, the land and the people yet to come.

Dombeck assumed he could count on support from the conservation community, since it was so vocal about protecting roadless areas, and because the moratorium idea had been floated a year or two before at a meeting among Anne Bartuska, Dombeck's assistant; Marty Hayden of Earthjustice; Jim Jontz of the Alliance for America; and Dominick DellaSala of the World Wildlife Fund, this according to DellaSala. The conservation community was united in its desire to preserve roadless areas and stop excessive road building. It had nearly succeeded in taking away the Forest Service's road budget. Now, with an ally in Mike Dombeck and new resources from Pew, via Audubon, and through Heritage Forests, it was poised to take the fight many steps further.

Jim Lyons, Dombeck's boss, thought a road-building moratorium made sense. He tells a story of being in Jackson Hole, Wyoming, for a meeting and taking an afternoon off to go fishing with a road engineer named Vaughan Stokes. They drove into Grand Teton National Park. After a while the pavement ended and they continued on a bumpy, rutted, washed-out track that was in dire need of attention. "We'd better tell the Park Service about this mess," Lyons said to Stokes. Stokes gently informed him that they had just left the park and were on Forest Service land. Lyons said from that moment on he was determined to do something to fix the road program in his department.

Lyons and Dombeck agreed that they would have to proceed cautiously, not let too many people in on the plan or it would be leaked and become a major political issue before it was thought through thoroughly. Secretary Glickman endorsed the idea as well. "We didn't want this to get out and become a public fight," Dombeck said. "A tenacious and volatile issue like this," he added, "if it becomes public, the issue gets taken away from you. Pretty soon Senator Stevens and Don Young are calling to say they want to be in on it. And the ultra greens too, and you've lost control. We limited the people who knew about it to twenty-five or fifty."

Eventually they had their plan ready. Toward the end of 1997, Dombeck placed courtesy calls to Senator Craig and Representative Smith to warn them of the upcoming announcement; they both tried to talk him out of going forward. Their vehement reactions convinced Dombeck that he was doing the right thing.

Dombeck announced the news on January 22, 1998, saying that he was instituting an eighteen-month "temporary suspension" of road building while they studied the situation and came up with a permanent solution. *Moratorium* seemed a little too forceful a word to begin with.

Senator Craig, as related by Mike Dombeck, though he'd been warned of what was afoot, shot off a press release that characterized the news as "a hand grenade rolled under my door." Mike Dombeck suspected that that line had been written by Mark Rey, who worked for the senator, had been a principal lobbyist for the timber industry for many years, and would later succeed Jim Lyons as agriculture under secretary, overseer of the Forest Service.

Rey is a wily, charming, and very effective operator. Much of the environmental community fears him, with good reason. Rey, like Lyons, has degrees in forestry and wildlife management. They speak the same language, but with radically different accents. In an interview, Rey denied authorship of the Craig quip. When asked if he had written the line, Rey said, "Not that particular one. I've written a lot of colorful quotes for senators that I've worked for as well as used them myself, but the 'hand grenade under the door' analogy was Craig's. He speaks that way often in terms of the legislative process. In fact, when I came down here [to the Department of Agriculture] he said, 'Your job will be completely different now.' I said, 'What do you mean?' and he said, 'Now you'll have to catch the hand grenades.'"

Mike Francis of The Wilderness Society had seen what was coming. "When you work in the Senate for twenty years, sitting across the table from politicians and bureaucrats, you learn to read upside-down," he said in an interview. "I was called in for a briefing by the Forest Service on what it was planning about roads. They discussed five steps they were planning to take to improve the situation. There was a sixth step they didn't mention, but I could read it on their list. It was to declare a moratorium."

Francis raced back to his office and slipped a few questions about roadless areas into a poll the society was just about to conduct. The first two were straightforward, what-do-you-think-about-roadless-areas questions. The next three added wildlife, water, and recreation. The results stunned him. Fully 60 percent of the public supported protecting roadless areas (he had thought the very idea too abstract to interest people). Adding in the other three values, the number rose above 70 percent. "We had the public with us," he said. "We just had to get it moving. It was the perfect example of the Tip O'Neill maxim to find out where the parade is going, then get out in front of it."

The moratorium by another name, however, was seriously lacking, in the view of the environmental community: it omitted any national forest that had finalized *revised forest plans.* This meant that nineteen forests in the Pacific Northwest—major producers of sawlogs—were not included, nor were a half-dozen small forests across the country. The Tongass National Forest was also omitted. The Tongass, at sixteen-plus million acres the biggest national forest by far, covers most of the Alaska panhandle and is prized not only for its big, old spruces, firs, and hemlocks, but also for its fjords to rival Norway's; five species of salmon that nearly choke its streams; brown bears and bald eagles in profusion; and deer and shellfish that, along with the salmon, provide subsistence to native Tlingits and other Americans, and support an important commercial fishery.

The Tongass has been hit hard by logging, both on the national forest and on adjacent Native lands, but it is still the wildest and most magnificent of the public's forests. To leave it out of the moratorium did not make sense. Biologically. It was the politics that were the problem. Both Alaska senators, Ted Stevens and Frank Murkowski, and the state's lone representative, Don Young, are powerful supporters of the timber industry. Administration officials said later that they always wanted to include the Tongass but had to wait for public support to build to the point where that would be politically feasible. The situation in Oregon, Washington, and California was similar, though less acute. Timber had once been king in those places, but its economic importance had declined considerably over the previous decade or more.

The Tongass had already seen its share of scuffles, most notably over Admiralty Island, just offshore from Juneau. The island is almost entirely roadless and has only one town, Angoon. It covers a million acres and has the world's densest concentration of brown—grizzly—bears and the world's densest year-round concentration of bald eagles as well. In the 1960s, the Forest Service entered into a fifty-year contract with U.S. Plywood, which would log all the big trees on the island and process them at a new pulp mill, to be built at Berner's Bay on the mainland north of Juneau. The Sierra Club, the Sitka Conservation Society, and a wildlife guide named Karl Lane filed suit. Litigation surged back and forth for two decades. Most of the island was eventually turned into a wilderness national monument. With very few roads. Two pulp mills were then operating—at Ketchikan and Sitka—exporting much of their output to Japan. Proponents of keeping roads out of roadless areas argued that there were still plenty of trees accessible from existing roads and that no new roads need be built.

Forest Service Chief Mike Dombeck had decided to omit the Tongass from the moratorium in order not to anger the powerful Alaska delegation, but down deep he knew the omission was illogical and wrong.

The administration, meanwhile, was also delighted at the public reaction to the temporary suspension. "The public support was tremendous. It really got the public's attention. Republicans predictably tended to oppose it, Democrats support it," Dombeck said. He quoted Will Rogers to explain the rationale: "If you're in a hole, stop digging."

He also pointed out what was actually at stake. The national forests provide about 4 percent of the lumber and pulp consumed annually in the

United States. Removing roadless areas from the timber base would reduce the amount of timber theoretically available from the national forests by a paltry 6 percent. The overall reduction in the theoretically available timber supply would then go down by two-tenths of 1 percent, an amount that was trivial in the overall picture.

Ken Rait, then head of the Heritage Forests Campaign, points out that, at that stage, the proposal would have stopped road building, not logging, and the campaign was insisting on a cessation to logging in roadless areas even if it was carried out by balloons, helicopters, or vehicles that can navigate forested land without roads.

Local impacts of a road-building moratorium would be severe in some isolated places, of course, but overall, the economic impact of the moratorium would be tiny. This wasn't about economics, it was about ideology. This was forcefully illustrated by an angry letter from Senators Frank Murkowski (Alaska) and Larry Craig (Idaho) and Representatives Don Young (Alaska) and Helen Chenoweth (Idaho) threatening to have Dombeck sacked. The Society of American Foresters (SAF) announced that it would launch an "ethics investigation" into Dombeck's involvement in the Roadless Rule's development. This caused Dombeck later to observe that

> *of all the issues and challenges I dealt with in my career, this incident was really the only time I was personally insulted, to learn that a "professional" society that I was a member of would investigate me for ethics infractions. To me this experience exemplified the dark side of politics. If "they" are opposed to a policy and can't win on the merits, they go after you personally. Basically, SAF picked up where [Helen] Chenoweth's House of Representatives Forest Resources Committee left off with the same investigation. Chenoweth's Committee also found no infractions and dropped their investigation.*

The timber industry in Wyoming, meanwhile, foreshadowing an avalanche of lawsuits, challenged the moratorium in court. A similar case was filed in Idaho. The Justice Department, with environmental-group allies that had intervened to defend the moratorium, argued that the suit was premature, that the moratorium was only temporary. The courts agreed and dismissed both cases.

As the review was going on, and public involvement increased, George Frampton, chair of the President's Council on Environmental Quality, and John Podesta, White House chief of staff, began to get interested. And pretty soon Bill Clinton did too. "I didn't know why and I didn't care," Dombeck said. "If we could get the president's support it would make all the difference."

More than a hundred members of Congress wrote to the president urging protection for roadless areas. Another key event, according to several participants and observers, came when forest activists buried the White House with a quarter-million emails over a single weekend in June 1999 and shut down the servers. At the regular White House staff meeting the following Monday, people were asking each other what in the world was going on.

A year and a half after Mike Dombeck announced his temporary road-building suspension, in October 1999, Bill Clinton stood before television cameras at Reddish Knob in the George Washington National Forest in Virginia and told the nation that he was ordering Mike Dombeck to come up with a policy for protecting unroaded areas on the nation's national forests. Permanently. Clinton had just survived the effort to impeach him, and he was clearly happy to be announcing something positive and of major dimensions:

> *This kind of land has been important to me since I was a boy, where I learned by walking the Ozark and Ouachita National Forests of my home state that national forests are more than a source of timber, they are places of renewal of the human spirit and our natural environment. At the dawn of the new century we have the opportunity to act on behalf of these forests in a way that honors the vision of our forbears, [Theodore] Roosevelt and [Gifford] Pinchot.*
>
> *Within our national forests there are large parcels of land that don't contain roads of any kind and, in most cases, never have. From the beautiful stretch of the Alleghenies that we see here to the old-growth canyonlands of the Tahoe National Forest, these areas represent some of the last, best unprotected wildland anywhere in our nation. They offer unparalleled opportunities for hikers, hunters, and anglers. They're absolutely critical to the survival of many endangered species.*
>
> *And I think it's worth pointing out they are also very often a source of clean and fresh water for countless communities. They are, therefore, our treasured inheritance.*

*Today, we launch one of the largest land preservation efforts in
America's history to protect these priceless, back country lands. The
Forest Service will prepare a detailed analysis of how best to preserve
our forests' large roadless areas, and then present a formal proposal to
do just that. The Forest Service will also determine whether similar protection is warranted for smaller roadless areas that have not yet been
surveyed.*

*Through this action, we will protect more than 40 million acres, 20
percent of the total forest land in America in the national forests—from
activities, such as new road construction which would degrade the land.
We will ensure that our grandchildren will be able to hike up to this
peak, that others like it across the country will also offer the same opportunities. We will assure that when they get to the top they'll be able to
look out on valleys like this, just as beautiful then as they are now.*

*We will live up to the challenge Theodore Roosevelt laid down a cen-
tury ago to leave this land even a better land for our descendants than it
is for us.*

*It is very important to point out that we are not trying to turn the
national forests into museums. Even as we strengthen protections, the
majority of our forests will continue to be responsibly managed for sus-
tainable timber production and other activities. We are, once again,
determined to prove that environmental protection and economic growth
can, and must, go hand in hand.*

*Let me give you an example, because I've seen a lot of people already
saying a lot of terrible things about what I'm doing today, and how it is
going to end the world as we know it. This initiative should have almost
no effect on timber supply. Only five percent of our country's timber
comes from the national forests. Less than five percent of the national
forests' timber is now being cut in roadless areas. We can easily adjust
our federal timber program to replace five percent of five percent, but we
can never replace what we might destroy if we don't protect these 40 million acres....*

*It is no longer necessary to grow a modern economy by destroying nat-
ural resources and putting more greenhouse gases into the atmosphere.
In fact, we can create more jobs by following a responsible path to sus-
tainable development. (Transcript provided by the White House.)*

The president took no questions after the speech. Note the forty-million-acre figure. The Tongass National Forest in Alaska was still being omitted from the proposal. For the activists, there was still important work to be done. Many reporters, having heard repeatedly from the forces pushing for protection for all roadless areas, tried to ask why the Tongass was not included in the directive to Dombeck.

Shortly after the speech, which brought tears to many eyes, according to several people who were there, Clinton wrote the following, in a formal memo, to Agriculture Secretary Dan Glickman:

> *Accordingly, I have determined that it is in the best interest of our Nation, and of future generations, to provide strong and lasting protection for these forests, and I am directing you to initiate administrative proceedings to that end.*
>
> *Specifically, I direct the Forest Service to develop, and propose for public comment, regulations to provide appropriate long-term protection for most or all of these currently inventoried "roadless" areas, and to determine whether such protection is warranted for any smaller "roadless" areas not yet inventoried. The public, and all interested parties, should have the opportunity to review and comment on the proposed regulations. In the final regulations, the nature and degree of protections afforded should reflect the best available science and a careful consideration of the full range of ecological, economic, and social values inherent in these lands.*

The fat was in the fire. "If an issue isn't partisan already, having the president take a stand will quickly make it partisan," Mike Dombeck said. Especially a president like Bill Clinton, who was so thoroughly detested by many Republicans.

Republicans weren't the only problem, however. According to Dombeck, about a quarter of the 120 forest supervisors thought the roadless initiative was a bad idea. The rest were all for it. They were sick and tired of the endless battles they endured over the roadless areas in their forests.

The president's announcement launched what's known as a *scoping* process, where the Forest Service, in this case, undertakes to gather public comments on what the scope of its proposed new rule or regulation should be.

The Heritage Forests Campaign swung into action. Mat Jacobson was one of a staff of six working for Ken Rait and Heritage Forests. Jacobson had worked briefly for the Forest Service in Oregon (he was fired for being too outspoken in opposition to clear-cutting) and was a well-seasoned organizer from stints doing forest-protection work in Vermont and Appalachia. Jacobson, in an interview, told the author he had said to Rait, "I need a car, a driver, and three months. There's already an army out there. We just need to get it organized."

He began by gathering contact information for every forest activist and group he could find across the country. With geographic information system (GIS) software, he plotted the locations of all his contacts on a map and determined where the densest clusters were. He then mapped out a route that would take him to the center of each cluster. Next, he sent messages to people in his target areas saying that he was coming to pay a call, hoping to help them prepare for the scoping hearings, and that it appeared as if there was a chance to do something really dramatic to save roadless areas.

There was some resistance: Pew's funding of the Heritage Forests Campaign was a bit of a hindrance. Pew was mistrusted by some people, seen as the rich organization trying to dictate policy for these groups toward its own ends. "I didn't dictate anything," Jacobson says, "I figured we could help groups get what they wanted with excellent results, or try for what we wanted and get mediocre results at best." A key, he said, and this extended to all the organizing and recruiting of allies over the next weeks and months, was to make this a positive, hopeful campaign. Many environmental efforts are, by necessity, trying to stop bad things from happening. In this case, they could sell hope, a positive vision—nearly sixty million acres that could be spared the bulldozer and the chainsaw. People could, and would, get fired up. There was the opportunity to save a large swath of vital, vulnerable land, and build a powerful, national, political force in the process.

The Heritage Forests Campaign provided postcards for activists to send to the Forest Service. It provided vans to take people to the hearings, and pizza to eat on the way. Lapel pins. Bumper stickers. And always it was the local people who were doing the planning.

The experts from The Technology Project, led by Rob Stuart, pioneered new electronic tricks—Internet banner ads, click-through ads on Yahoo, ads that people could send to their friends and colleagues (so-called viral ads). They put together a listserv, one of the first uses of that now commonplace technique for quick, broadscale communication. "We could learn from mistakes," Jacobson says. At one of the early hearings in North Carolina, the proroadless activists threw a fish fry to attract participants. It ran overtime and they were late to the hearing. The prologging forces had signed up for the early speaking slots, and when the proroadless people got their chance to speak, the television cameras and reporters had all gone home. For the next hearing, in Missoula, Montana, the timber industry had sent truckers to pack the hall, first providing a meal at "the world's largest picnic table." So the proroadless activists got to the hearing room early, filled all the chairs, and signed up for all the speaking slots. The truckers were reduced to chanting slogans outside, on the street. The media representatives reported that the timber industry representatives chose to demonstrate outside and not participate in the hearing.

From his perch in Oregon, Ken Rait held weekly conference calls with activists all across the country as Heritage Forests signed up scores more campaign partners. They commissioned polls and held focus groups to hone their message, that is, to ensure that the way they talked about protecting roadless areas would be as persuasive as possible to as broad a public as possible. They placed ads in newspapers and on radio and television and sent envoys to meet with newspaper editorial boards. They also kept up a steady barrage of news releases reporting the results of polls and surveys; the results of scientific studies; and the contents of letters signed by religious leaders, business interests, scientists, and others.

The June 1999 letter to the administration urging protection for roadless areas had many more Democratic signers than Republican ones, so Rait decided to do some carefully targeted polling. He commissioned the White House's pollster, Mark Mellman, to measure general support for the idea of protecting roadless areas. Not surprisingly, he found solid support. So, seven months later, Rait commissioned Linda DiVall, a Republican pollster, head of the firm American Viewpoint, to gauge support for protection, and these results surprised everyone: nationwide she found 76 percent of those polled in support of roadless area protection. Among Republicans, those in favor of support came in at two to one. The polls, in turn, were used in mailings to editorial boards and as the basis for advertisements, including one printed in the *Washington Times*, that Republican bastion, headlined "Forest Protection Is for ~~Liberals~~ Conservatives":

It's no surprise when liberals support environmental protection. But you may be surprised to know that protecting roadless areas in our National Forests enjoys overwhelming support from conservatives and Republicans too.

According to a new survey by pollster Linda DiVall, a two-to-one majority of Republicans (62%–31%) supports the proposed plan to permanently protect all remaining roadless areas in our National Forests.

Who understands conservation better than conservatives? (3-10-2000)

The Heritage Forests Campaign signed the ad along with Republicans for Environmental Protection.

In the end, the scoping hearings—there were nearly two hundred—garnered about a quarter-million comments, by far the most ever, for such a process. Well over 90 percent of them urged protection for all roadless areas.

Why a Roadless Rule?

4

THE NEXT STEP, once the moratorium was in place and the Clinton directive made public, was to draft a rule, an executive order, a regulation, maybe a law, and submit it to the public for comment. It would need an analysis of its environmental impact and a suggestion of alternative methods of achieving the desired result. The administration knew it would be controversial and that it would have to survive legal challenges. They brought in teams of lawyers to make sure that every possible line of attack was anticipated and accommodated, that the rule complied with every applicable law.

There was no consensus, in fact, on whether the Forest Service had the legal authority to impose a rule that would ban road building in roadless areas. Some argued that Congress would have to enact such a law, a remote prospect at best with the political climate that prevailed toward the end of the Clinton administration. Clinton had been tried before the House of Representatives for allegedly lying under oath in the Monica Lewinsky matter, and though he had survived, he was wounded and deeply unpopular with a substantial fraction of the public and the Congress. Therefore, Congress did not seem a friendly venue for securing protection for roadless areas.

Steve Kallick of the Pew Charitable Trusts was reading a history of the Forest Service and was intrigued to learn how the saving of wilderness began. In the 1930s, Bob Marshall and Aldo Leopold persuaded the Forest Service to set aside particularly sensitive and valuable areas as primitive areas. The legal authority for this derived from the Forest Service's Organic Act—the law that created the agency in 1897—the same act cited years later by Earthjustice attorney Jim Angell in Judge Brimmer's courtroom. That law says that the secretary of agriculture is empowered to issue rules to protect the forests. This authority was confirmed and reinforced by the Multiple-Use Sustained-Yield Act of 1960. The key language in that law says, "The establishment and maintenance of areas of wilderness are consistent with the purposes and provisions of this Act" (see appendix 3). If the law provided legal authority for the Forest Service to protect wild areas, then it could still do so today, Kallick reasoned.

He was particularly interested in this possibility given his frustration with the slow progress in getting wilderness areas established state by state. There had been a flurry of wilderness bills enacted during the Reagan administration, but very little since then. Sticking with the area-by-area approach gave too much power to antiwilderness forces, which are well organized and have their local economic interests to defend, he thought. "We needed to take the fight to the other side," he said in an interview, and "force them to explain why they wanted to destroy these last, best places." He figured a national campaign to protect a broad swath of unprotected wildlands could not only succeed, but could also build a powerful new coalition of organizations throughout the country. "Environmentalists working on saving forests were balkanized by the Forest Service's planning process," he says. "We needed some sort of national push."

They also needed allies. Officials in the administration were skeptical, as were some potential allies in the environmental community. According to Kallick, it was Niel Lawrence of the Natural Resources Defense Council who sold environmentalists on the idea that a national rule, put forward by the executive branch, was possible, advisable, and legal.

To get the administration to embrace this approach, it was necessary to demonstrate overwhelming public support, which would convince the White House that this was a fight it could win and use to burnish its legacy. Indeed, during the scoping process, the Heritage Forests Campaign produced a large poster leaning heavily on the legacy angle: "President Clinton's bold step is one of the largest and most significant land conservation actions ever imagined, let alone deployed. It should be embraced and celebrated by all Americans." John Podesta, the new White House chief of staff, asked Ken Rait if Heritage

Forests could stimulate as many comments and as much support for a national rule as it had during the scoping process. Rait said yes.

Rait's colleague, Mat Jacobson, has a theory about winning public campaigns like this one. Jacobson draws a pyramid on a scrap of paper, with three or four horizontal lines across it. The pyramid represents the public. The bottom slice stands for the fraction of the public that is least engaged in a particular issue; the point on top denotes those who care most passionately. A general public opinion poll, he explains, will tell you that more than 90 percent of the public supports protection for roadless areas, for example. But way at the top, where you find the passionate environmentalists and the organized loggers and the antienvironment ideologues, the split will be closer to fifty-fifty. And this is where most decisions get made, because those people make the most noise and are best organized.

The Heritage Forests Campaign's goal—the goal of all the organizations working to save roadless areas—was, and is, to increase the influence of the second tier of the public, where support for protection has a far greater majority. And the strategy to do this is to persuade newspapers to write editorials in favor of, in this case, protection for roadless areas, including those in Alaska, which will impress policy makers and the public alike. Also, probably more important, get the story on television, where a growing fraction of the public gets its news. The more vocal and engaged the middle ranks become, the better chance that the decision makers will listen.

On May 9, 2000, the Forest Service released its proposal in the form of a draft environmental impact statement (DEIS), seven hundred pages long, along with a proposed rule for the protection of roadless areas, inviting further public comment over the space of sixty-nine days. The DEIS included the Pacific Northwest forests (at the urging of Senators Patty Murray of Washington, Ron Wyden of Oregon, and Max Baucus of Montana; and Governors Gary Locke of Washington and John Kitzhaber of Oregon) plus the other forests left out of the earlier proposal (see chapter 3), but it still excluded the Tongass National Forest and was widely denounced by the conservation community for that fatal flaw. It also failed to ban logging by helicopter and other techniques that do not require roads. Environmental forces argued that it did not live up to the vision President Clinton had outlined on Reddish Knob. A particularly scathing pamphlet put out by Heritage Forests was headlined "An American Legacy: Forests Aren't Protected by a Stump Speech":

On May 9, 2000, the U.S. Forest Service issued a draft environmental impact statement [that] ... will still allow 73 percent of all logging to continue in [roadless areas].... The Forest Service is clearly deaf to the will of the American people. The fate of our last wild forests now rests in the hands of the American people and the President of the United States.

Television ads in the same vein appeared. The plan was to turn up the heat on the Forest Service and force inclusion of the Tongass. Newspapers across the country, which had received a steady diet of press releases, fact sheets, poll results, and the like from Heritage Forests and its member groups for months, weighed in with editorials, the vast majority favoring the proposal but wanting it strengthened. Here are some sample editorial statements:

- "Dealing with the Tongass is tricky, but its wild areas are no less deserving of protection. As it moves to a final plan, the Forest Service ought to do better on this one." *Washington Post:* May 13, 2000.

- "Clinton is correct in calling for a ban on new road construction in roadless areas of this country's national forests. But the President did not go far enough.... We only wish he had included the Tongass, the largest forest of all." *Houston Chronicle:* May 10, 2000.

- "There's a lot less than meets the eye in President Clinton's roadless proposal for national forests. Less protection for wildlands than advertised by the president." *Seattle Post-Intelligencer:* May 14, 2000.

- "The Clinton administration's plan for our national forests' roadless areas is itself a dead-end. The draft plan the Clinton team recently released first seems to ban new road building in all roadless areas. But the proposal creates so many exceptions, even fudging the definition of what a roadless area is, it may accomplish nothing." *Denver Post:* May 23, 2000.

One difficulty that had plagued the environmental community more or less constantly over many decades was that there were groups saying many different things on the same subject, that is, there was a lack of what has come to be called *message discipline.* Stories abounded of frustrated reporters trying to get the conservationists' view on a given subject and hearing contradictory cacophony.

The constant roadless conference calls and meetings, however, had brought the wildly disparate groups together to the point where the *Sacramento Bee* would editorialize, speaking of the proroadless groups' comments on the DEIS, that "However different the voices, the song sounded as if it were sung out of a single hymnal" (May 12, 2000). Ken Rait ruefully commented in a June 16 memo to his allies, "I can't remember a time the environmental community was criticized by the media for such message discipline. Oh well. Damned if you do, damned if you don't." Mat Jacobson of the Heritage Forests Campaign includes the line on his resume, as a matter of pride.

The Forest Service scheduled another four hundred-plus public meetings over the next two-plus months, two at each of the 155 national forests and nearby towns, as well as in major cities.

The grassroots network, well trained and organized through its scoping experience, went back to work. Vans were hired, pizza ordered, volunteers recruited. Mat Jacobson and company were afraid they might be overwhelmed at hearings in remote sites near western national forests, but the organizing and recruiting—not to mention the public's enthusiasm for roadless areas—worked. The proroadless forces outnumbered prologging forces at every hearing.

The U.S. Public Interest Research Group (PIRG), led by Gene Karpinski, armed its canvassers with preaddressed postcards urging the Forest Service to ban roads, logging, and mining on all national forests immediately. The Pew Charitable Trusts had underwritten this effort as well, via contributions to the National Audubon Society, so the canvassers were not asking for money as they knocked on doors nationwide; they were simply providing a convenient way for citizens to make their views known to their government. It was the most successful canvass in PIRG history—its field people kept running out of postcards. People who answered the doors they knocked on were mostly enthusiastic about supporting roadless-area protection.

The comments favored the Roadless Rule by about twenty to one, with most urging inclusion of the Tongass. A spirited debate bubbled along among people in the Forest Service and the Agriculture Department over the Tongass. Some argued that to bend to the will of the conservation movement would show weakness. Others argued that it would simply be democracy in action. Why solicit public comment if you're not willing to reconsider what you're proposing? This, after all, is the purpose of all this public participation as mandated by the National Environmental Policy Act. Proponents of the status quo argued that such decisions should not be popularity contests. Proponents of change replied that if the process were seen as pro forma window dressing, the process itself would be perverted.

Over the next few months, and counting previous comment periods, a total of more than 1.6 million comments were received by the agency, by far the most ever in the country's history. (The previous record had been set when comments were gathered concerning the definition of *organic* for new food-labeling regulations. Those comments numbered about 250,000.)

Then came the election of 2000 and Al Gore's crushing defeat at the hands of the Supreme Court. If the Clinton administration had thought it could await a Gore administration to put the finishing touches on the rule, it quickly changed its mind.

A week after the election, the Forest Service released its final environmental impact statement. The combination of overwhelming public pressure, newspaper editorials, and the fact that Mike Dombeck, Jim Lyons, and others wanted to include the Tongass in the Roadless Rule all along had won the day. The final environmental impact statement proclaimed that the Roadless Area Conservation Rule would apply to all roadless areas on all national forests, including the Tongass.

Even now, there was still one nagging compromise—the Tongass would remain open to road building and roadless-area logging for four years, to provide a transition for loggers and mill hands. Niel Lawrence of the Natural Resources Defense Council remarked, "Unfortunately, the timber industry is gearing up right now to clear-cut more Tongass roadless areas, so America's last great rainforest can't wait four or five more years for protection." Marty Hayden of Earthjustice agreed: "It would not be prudent to leave the world's largest remaining temperate rainforest open to potential pillaging for a few years. While we are pleased the Forest Service has recognized the importance of the Tongass to all Americans, it must now be awarded immediate protection to ensure this unique treasure will be enjoyed by future generations."

The proroadless leadership quickly huddled. Marty Hayden tells of mapping out an ad campaign on a paper napkin in a restaurant in Anchorage with, among others, Deborah Williams and Matt Zencey of the Alaska Rainforest

Campaign. They concluded that they'd have to go after Bill Clinton directly, to appeal to his desire for a green legacy. They sketched out an ad—both print and television versions—on the theme "Only a President Could Save a Forest. Only a Great One Would."

That ad, sponsored by the Alaska Rainforest Campaign, and another developed by Earthjustice, ran more than nine hundred times on tiny cable outlets in the Washington, DC, area they thought the president might see. It ran in newspapers he might be expected to scan, including the *New York Times* and the *Washington Post*. They even explored the idea of buying TV time or newspaper space in Hanoi during a presidential visit there but had to drop the idea for practical reasons. And all the groups urged their members to send one more volley to the White House demanding that the Roadless Rule apply to the Tongass immediately.

On January 5, 2001, Clinton and Glickman announced that they were going to adopt the Roadless Area Conservation Rule and ban further road building in roadless areas of the national forest system.

Three days later the timber company Boise Cascade filed a suit to challenge the law in a federal court in Idaho, alleging violation of seven federal laws, including the National Environmental Policy Act, the National Forest Management Act, the Administrative Procedure Act, the Organic Act, the Multiple-Use Sustained-Yield Act, the Wilderness Act, and the Omnibus Consolidated Appropriations Act of 1997.

Boise Cascade was joined by the Blue Ribbon Coalition (an organization that promotes the use of motorized off-road vehicles on public lands and is supported financially by snowmobile manufacturers and other such enterprises), several snowmobile associations, two livestock companies, and the Kootenai tribe of Idaho. A day later, the State of Idaho filed its own suit with the same allegations. The two challenges were quickly consolidated.

The Idaho suits claimed that the rule was illegal because there had been insufficient opportunity for public involvement in the creation of the rule; that communities near the national forests should have more to say about management of the forests because they are more dependent on them than others; that the rule as written was not sufficiently flexible; and that the rule would cause "irreparable harm" to various vital economic interests and to the forests themselves by precluding various sorts of "management activities," such as pest control and thinning for fire protection. This last claim would be vigorously disputed by the environmental intervenors, who would argue that protecting land from roads, mining, and logging could hardly be construed as harming them.

On January 12, 2001, the final rule appeared in the *Federal Register*. It said, among many other things, that "the size of the existing forest road system and attendant budget constraints prevent the agency from managing its road system to the safety and environmental standards to which it was built." It also observed that "inventoried roadless areas [IRAS] provide clean drinking water and function as biological strongholds for populations of threatened and endangered species." It referred to the huge maintenance backlog and spoke of the devastating landslides that have occurred when abandoned roads wash away: "Of 1,290 landslides reviewed in 41 sub watersheds [in Oregon and Washington] 52% were related to roads, 31% to timber harvest, and 17% occurred in undisturbed forest." It defined a road as "a motor vehicle travelway over 50 inches wide, unless designated and managed as a trail." It spoke of all the protected species of plants and animals that depend on the unroaded areas of the forests, including areas that would be vital for the recovery of species like the grizzly bear.

The rule further stated that "road construction, reconstruction, and timber harvesting activities can result in fragmentation of ecosystems, the introduction of non-native invasive species, and other adverse consequences to the health and integrity of inventoried roadless areas."

Anticipating a legal argument that would be hurled against the rule, the text said, "The Roadless Area Conservation rule, unlike the establishment of wilderness areas, will allow a multitude of activities including motorized uses, grazing, and oil and gas development that does not require new roads to continue in inventoried roadless areas." Further, the rule allowed "construction in inventoried roadless areas when a road is needed to protect public health and safety in cases of an imminent threat of flood, fire, or other catastrophic event." And, it pointed out that "building roads into inventoried roadless areas would likely increase the chance of human-caused fires due to the increased presence of people."

Fire had long been used as an excuse to overharvest the forests. A series of dry years beginning around the time the Roadless Rule controversy was raging would thrust fire to center stage, while at the same time, a deluge of studies of the likely consequences of global warming suggested that drought and attendant fire would remain a serious and growing problem.

And finally, the rule addressed the matter most important to the environmental organizations: "The final rule applies immediately to the Tongass National Forest but adopts a mitigation measure that both assures long-term protection and a smooth transition for forest-dependent communities."

The mitigation measure was a grandfather clause for a few timber sales that had already been announced in the *Federal Register* and was a sop to the Alaska congressional delegation, which was united in vociferous opposition to the very idea of the Roadless Rule. They immediately pointed out that including the Tongass was not among the alternatives suggested by the DEIS and argued that including that vast forest was improper, if not downright illegal.

In sum, the notice argued that the Roadless Rule would protect air and water quality, enhance biological diversity, benefit fish and wildlife, provide recreation opportunities, and thereby lessen pressure on existing wilderness areas, reduce the risk of invasive species, save money, and "set an example for the global community."

It would also trigger legal battles of epic proportions.

The Untold Story of the Pew Charitable Trusts 5

JOSHUA REICHERT grew up in northern California in the mid-1900s and put himself through winemaking school at the University of California at Davis, working weekends and holidays in Central Valley fields alongside migrant laborers from Mexico, mostly, and from Central America. Following graduation, he went to work as an organizer for the United Farmworkers Union (UFW), Caesar Chavez's organization. The famous boycott of table grapes and lettuce had forced growers to allow workers to vote on whether to unionize. Elections were being held at farms throughout the valley, and growers were working hard to discourage workers from opting for the UFW. Reichert traveled from farm to farm to ensure that the elections were open and fair and that no undue pressure was exerted on the workers to force them to vote against the union.

During college, Reichert had also worked with Native American groups in the West and, following that interest, he earned a doctorate in anthropology at Princeton. He taught for a year at Duke, then accepted a fellowship with the American Association for the Advancement of Science, working on Capitol Hill for a year. He then worked for a number of years for the InterAmerican Foundation, helping indigenous groups in Latin America. He served as executive vice president for Conservation International, then worked for a time at the National Security Archive, an invaluable organization that throws light into the shadowy recesses of American domestic and foreign policy. Joshua Reichert is a man of many talents and broad experience, in other words.

In the early 1990s, Reichert was recruited to head up a small section dealing with the environment for the Pew Charitable Trusts. The trusts were established in 1948 by four children of Joseph Pew, the founder of Sun Oil. Where once the trusts had underwritten conservative causes, a younger generation—Joseph Pew's grandchildren—was moving into leadership positions and nudging the trusts to widen and liberalize their horizons. Reichert was asked to write a report with recommendations on what the trusts might support in the environmental field. He seemed a good choice. His experience with farmworkers had made him aware of the dangers pesticides posed to workers and wildlife. His work in Latin America had shown how bad environmental policies and practices had resulted in deleterious impacts on people and the environment.

Reichert's assignment was to create a white paper outlining what Pew could do to make a difference over the next five to ten years. His first recommendation was that it focus on policy work rather than on-the-ground projects, with an emphasis on national policies and some state and regional efforts. The white paper recommended concentration in 5 areas: climate, with a focus on electricity generation; transportation and appliance and building efficiency, with the general purpose of reducing carbon emissions (a decade and a half before Al Gore's *An Inconvenient Truth* [1992], don't forget); protection for large tracts of intact wilderness, concentrating on public rather than private land for practical purposes; toxic chemicals; and population. The toxics program lasted until the mid-1990s, then was discontinued. The population program was a response to the Mexico City Policy, a vestige of the Reagan years, which required that nongovernmental organizations receiving federal funds promise not to perform or advocate abortions in foreign countries. That program was spun off to another corner of the trusts. The Mexico City Policy was rescinded by President Clinton very early in his presidency but reinstated by President George W. Bush in 2001, the day after he was inaugurated.

Reichert started in 1990 with a staff of one and a budget of around $2 million. The trusts were governed by the rules that cover foundations, which meant no lobbying, no campaigns, no political or legislative activities of any sort. All the work to support the campaigns had to be quiet and at arm's length. Pew would provide funds for permitted activities, to the National

Audubon Society, in this case, but it would not take a leading, public role itself. Pew would not begin to step out of the shadows for a decade or more.

In 2004, however, came a big change. The Pew Charitable Trusts ceased being a foundation, in the categories established by the Internal Revenue Service and other agencies that oversee not-for-profit enterprises, and became instead a public charity, not so very different, as Reichert describes it, from the Natural Resources Defense Council or other environmental organizations.

Pew was different in one vital respect, however—it had an endowment of something like $5 billion. As of early 2008, according to Reichert, the Pew Environmental Program had a budget of $70 million, offices in twenty-five states, plus Australia, New Zealand, and several European countries, and the largest campaign staff of any environmental organization in the country. But we get ahead of ourselves.

The key to all these campaigns, Reichert says, is organizing people, helping them get involved in public discourse and find leverage points to make a difference in public policy decisions.

Early on, back in the early 1990s, while Pew was still a quiet player in the background, it undertook projects in the Pacific Northwest, the Southwest, and the Southeast. The idea was to bring together local and regional groups with common interests, help them forge common agendas, and help pay the bills. "It was a different model than these groups were used to," Reichert said in a phone interview in early 2008. "Building coalitions in the environmental business is not necessarily a natural act." In most small groups, people are working on ten things at once. No one can devote full time to a single campaign. Pew hired organizers to concentrate on protection of old-growth forests in the Pacific Northwest, for example, to coordinate and assist small groups scattered all across the region. The effort was careful and methodical and paid some dividends, though progress was modest and incremental. They were constantly on the lookout for a bold national campaign that could build the movement and save large tracts of land nationwide.

In the early 1990s, Pew convened meetings around the country with the aim of building a nationwide, unified forest campaign. It was a disaster. According to Steve Kallick, who now runs a campaign aimed at protecting wildlands in Canada, at least two of the meetings ended in fisticuffs. One group said the only campaign that made sense was one to ban all logging on all national forests. Period. Another group said that anything beyond a campaign to end clear-cutting was too radical. The effort was abandoned as premature. I spent an afternoon earlier this year (April 11) with Kallick, Rait, and Jacobson. I spent a couple of hours earlier (February 18) with Kallick, and an evening with Jacobson in DC on January 16, 2008. These quotes come from those conversations.

Steve Kallick is a lawyer who started his legal career at the Sierra Club Legal Defense Fund (now Earthjustice) in Juneau, Alaska, in 1982. He helped win several big suits aimed at stopping the overcutting of the Tongass National Forest, along the way helping to build alliances with Native Alaskan organizations. After his stint at the Legal Defense Fund, Kallick was recruited into the Southeast Alaska Conservation Coalition (SEACC), where he remained for five years. As he tells the story, the environmental community, with major help from Congressman George Miller and others, managed to persuade Congress to enact the Tongass Timber Reform Act, which set aside 300,000 acres of wilderness on the forest. "We thought we had won," he says, "but the next year the Forest Service offered the biggest timber sales that had ever been offered on the forest." Kallick left SEACC to go to work on the staff of Representative Michael Finkelstein in the statehouse in Juneau.

In 1992, when the Pew expansion was getting under way, Josh Reichert, along with representatives from the Mott Foundation, the Rockefeller Brothers Fund, and one or two others, called a meeting among groups interested in Southeast Alaska and the Tongass National Forest. The idea was to spark creation of a new coalition to fight for the forest and to prime the pump with serious money. "I was afraid all that money would make everybody crazy," Kallick says (he was on the board of SEACC at this time), but he agreed to become the first head of the Pew-funded Alaska Rainforest Campaign, a coalition comprising SEACC, Audubon Alaska, the Alaska Center for the Environment, the Alaska Coalition, the Alaska Wilderness League, Defenders of Wildlife, Earthjustice, the Eyak Preservation Council, the National Wildlife Federation, the Natural Resources Defense Council, the Sierra Club, the Sitka Conservation Society, the U.S. Public Interest Research Group, and The Wilderness Society.

There was a renewed effort to slow down logging on the Tongass, with particular focus on two fifty-year logging contracts that were like life sentences for the forest, guaranteeing a steady oversupply of logs to large pulp mills at Sitka and Ketchikan. A relentless campaign of lobbying and litigation resulted in the closing of both mills and the cancellation of both contracts by the end of the century.

By 1996, Steve Kallick was planning to resign from the Rainforest Campaign. Josh Reichert phoned to say that Tom Wathen, head of the environment program at Pew, was leaving his position and asked if Kallick would be interested in applying for it. He was flattered but apprehensive. The mighty Pew Charitable Trusts of Philadelphia were a far cry from the rough and tumble of Juneau: "I wasn't sure a rube from the sticks with long red hair and a bushy beard would fit in." But he accepted the offer, and relocated to Philadelphia.

While Kallick acknowledges his role in dreaming up the idea of a nation-wide roadless campaign, he gives much credit to Niel Lawrence of the Natural Resources Defense Council and the late Jim Jontz, who served from 1986 to 1992 in the House of Representatives from Indiana, where he was a major environmental champion, especially in efforts to protect ancient forests in the Pacific Northwest.

Marty Hayden argues that by the time the Heritage Forests Campaign was created, the national environmental movement, led by the Natural Resources Defense Council, the Sierra Club, The Wilderness Society, Earthjustice, and others, had agreed on their goal—a national rule to protect roadless areas. Pew's money and organizing push would help it happen, in a big way. Sorting out who deserves credit for the conception and execution of the various pieces of this saga is all but impossible. Fortunately, there's plenty of credit to go around.

The Rule Goes Final, the Lawsuits Fly 6

A SCANT WEEK before the Clinton administration gave way to the George W. Bush regime, the Roadless Area Conservation Rule became the law of the land, to become effective sixty days following publication of the formal notice in the *Federal Register*, that is, on March 12, 2001.

No sooner had George W. Bush promised Chief Justice William Rehnquist and the rest of the world that he would uphold the Constitution than the president's new chief of staff, Andrew Card, issued a memorandum to all the executive agencies to freeze any rules issued recently by the Clinton administration. The Roadless Rule was one of those. Its effective date was pushed back to May 12, 2001. Ironically, the authority cited for the issuance of the memo, titled "Regulatory Review Plan," was Executive Order 12866, issued in 1993 by Bill Clinton.

The ostensible reason for the freeze was to give the new administration time to review the rules to see if they were reasonable, legal, and appropriate. An exhaustive investigation by the staff of the Senate Government Affairs Committee, then chaired by Senator Joe Lieberman of Connecticut, however, carried out in 2002, determined that, with respect to the Roadless Rule, "the Bush administration appears to have pre-determined that the regulations should be changed, and sought to employ whatever tools and tactics it deemed convenient to effect that change." The Lieberman report went on to say that

> one would hope . . . the new administration would carefully review the rule, the data supporting it, and undertake to revise it only if there appeared to be a rational basis for doing so, within the requirements of the applicable statutes. Based on the documents provided by the agencies, however, it appears no such review was undertaken . . . . [The documents reviewed] contain nothing that could be considered work product, analysis, research, or narrative reflecting a systematic review of either the substance or procedure associated with promulgation of the final rule.
>
> In place of a focus on whether the rule should be modified, the administration concerned itself with tactics. The documents reviewed contained proposals and option papers discussing tactically how to achieve the desired result—an overturning of the rule as written. The preferred result was to replace the rule with a return to the traditional decisionmaking by local Forest Service officials. In other words, it appears that a predetermination had been made that the new national requirements were wrong and should be reversed—the issue for the department was how to achieve that goal. (Rewriting the Rules, Report prepared by the majority staff of the Committee on Government Affairs, U.S. Senate, 2002.)

The investigation found that the new administration put forward three options: extend the effective date beyond March 12, and remove the rule later without a public comment period; rescind the rule immediately, with no public comment period; or rescind the rule immediately and put forward a new rule. In the end, the first option was adopted (delay the effective date of the rule) with a modification of the third (leave the rule in place, defend it only nominally, and replace it later).

There was a companion strategy as well, which involved the litigation filed to challenge the rule. Idaho Governor Dirk Kempthorne, who would go on to become secretary of the interior toward the end of the George W. Bush administration, wrote to Secretary of Agriculture Ann Veneman describing the state's legal challenge and asked that his negotiating team be allowed to brief her staff, a meeting that was held on February 27, 2001.

Soon after, it became clear that the administration would not defend the Roadless Rule with much vigor in court. As the Lieberman investigation observed, "USDA officials were all too happy to have the court take the blame for a decision that the administration itself supported, but was not willing to take the heat for having made." Or, as the report concluded, the Forest Service had decided to "let a judge take the rule down."

The environmental organizations that had put so much effort into helping create the rule and then drumming up public support for it, however, were not going to let it go without a fight. The first order of business was to intervene in pending and expected lawsuits. At this point, attorneys for the environmental groups stepped forward.

Earthjustice produced an informal team of attorneys as the rule was challenged in far-flung courtrooms. Patti Goldman and Kristen Boyles had helped get early challenges dismissed as not yet *ripe*, that is, no decisions had yet been made that were definite enough for a court to review. Once the Idaho cases were filed, Doug Honnold and Tim Preso filed motions to intervene on behalf of Idaho Rivers United, the Idaho Conservation League, The Wilderness Society, the Sierra Club, the Natural Resources Defense Council, the Pacific Rivers Council, and Defenders of Wildlife. They argued in their opening brief that the groups and their members used roadless areas in the national forests and therefore had a right to participate in the cases. "The remaining National Forest roadless areas are among our country's environmental treasures," they wrote, and "roadless areas are pristine portions of the National Forests as yet untouched by roadbuilding, logging, or other developments. These lands are among the last vestiges of the great wild continent that Europeans first found in North America. Today they are critical to our nation's ecological health."

There are two bases on which parties may be allowed to intervene in a federal civil lawsuit. One is *by right*, meaning that their interest is so compelling that they clearly must be permitted to participate in the case. The second route is at the judge's discretion, known as *permissive intervention*. Judge Lodge ruled that the organizations qualified under both standards.

On January 31, 2001, the State of Alaska filed a suit in district court in that state to challenge the rule. Immediately Earthjutice attorneys Eric Jorgensen and Tom Waldo filed intervention papers on behalf of the Sitka Conservation Society, the Southeast Alaska Conservation Council, the Alaska Center for the Environment, The Wilderness Society, and the National Audubon Society. The motion was unopposed.

A week later, Secretary Veneman announced that the effective date of the rule would be postponed two more months, until May 12, as directed by Andrew Card, the new White House chief of staff. She hinted that changes were in the works, and that, in the interim, the forests would be managed with the guidance of five principles:

- *Make informed decisions to ensure that inventoried roadless area [IRA] management is implemented with reliable information and accurate mapping, including local expertise and experience.*
- *Work with states, tribes, local communities, and the public through a process that is fair, open, and responsive to local input and information.*
- *Protect forests to ensure that the potential negative effects of severe wildfire, insect, and disease activity are addressed.*
- *Protect communities, homes, and property from the risk of severe wildfire and other risks on adjacent federal lands.*
- *Ensure that states, tribes, and private citizens who own property within inventoried roadless areas have access to their property as required by existing law. (www.roadless.fs.fed.us)*

Conservation groups noted the complete lack of anything about preserving ecological integrity, biodiversity, wildlife habitat, watershed health, or recreational opportunities.

On April 20, the State of Utah filed suit challenging the rule. Earthjustice attorney Jim Angell moved to intervene on behalf of the Southern Utah Wilderness Alliance, The Wilderness Society, the Sierra Club, the Pacific Rivers Council, the Natural Resources Defense Council, the National Audubon Society, and Defenders of Wildlife. On the same day, the timber industry filed two suits to challenge the rule in Washington, DC. Doug Honnold and Tim Preso intervened on behalf of The Wilderness Society, the Sierra Club, the Pacific Rivers Council, and the Oregon Natural Resources Council, now known as Oregon Wild.

On May 8, four North Dakota counties filed yet another suit challenging the rule. Todd True, of the Earthjustice office in Seattle, moved to intervene in this one, on behalf of the Sierra Club, The Wilderness Society, the Pacific Rivers Council, the Natural Resources Defense Council, Defenders of Wildlife, the National Audubon Society, the National Wildlife Federation, and the North Dakota Wildlife Federation. On May 19, the State of Wyoming filed its own suit challenging the rule. Jim Angell quickly intervened on behalf of the Wyoming Outdoor Council, The Wilderness Society, Biodiversity Associates, the Pacific Rivers Council, the Natural Resources Defense Council, the National Audubon Society, and Defenders of Wildlife. And finally, on September 10, 2001, the State of North Dakota jumped in with yet another suit, again attracting the same intervenors that had joined the earlier North Dakota suit, again represented by Todd True. In all, nine suits had been filed to challenge the rule. The environmentalists would battle each and every one.

The suits varied somewhat in their details, but there were many similarities. They all argued that the Roadless Area Conservation Rule, as published in the *Federal Register*, violated the National Environmental Policy Act in that there had not been sufficient time and opportunity for the public to let its views be known, and that the range of alternatives examined in the environmental review process was too limited. Some alleged violations of the Wilderness Act and the Administrative Procedure Act. All asked that the rule be held illegal and blocked from taking effect.

Meanwhile, John Ashcroft had been nominated to the office of U.S. attorney general, the nation's chief lawyer responsible for defending the United States and its Constitution, laws, rules, agencies, and regulations, and for prosecuting federal lawbreakers. At Ashcroft's confirmation hearing on January 19, 2001, Maria Cantwell, the newly elected Democratic senator from Washington, zeroed in on the Roadless Rule, and asked whether Ashcroft, a former senator from Missouri, would defend the rule: "It may be that the president-elect opposes that policy," she said [Bush had, in fact, opposed the proposed rule during the campaign], "but you, as attorney general—and there are court cases already now being filed in challenge to that administrative... to the roadless area policy that has now been implemented by this Administrative Procedure Act. So even if the president-elect is opposed to that policy, will you, as the enforcement agency underneath your office, enforce and uphold that law and defend those cases?"

Ashcroft answered, "Well, I will, regardless of whether or not I supported something as a senator, defend the rule. And if it is a rule with the force and effect of law, I will defend those cases."

Cantwell: "Even if the president might be seeking a new administrative overturn of that?"

Ashcroft: "I think if the president wants to change the law, he has to follow the law in order to do so."

Cantwell: "Okay."

Ashcroft: "And I will support and enforce the law. I think that's the responsibility, and I think that's what I've promised to do. I can't be result-oriented, I have to be law-oriented. And I think I would disserve the president and the country were I to do otherwise."

It was reassuring to the environmental groups, but the promise was not to last very long.

The Economic and Spiritual Value of Roadless Areas 7

THE RATIONALE for opening roadless areas to logging and mining is often couched in terms of jobs and economic prosperity. But roadless areas have values other than for lumber, pulp, oil, gas, and hard rock minerals. Many studies have attempted to measure the economic value of wilderness, whether it's formal wilderness areas or unprotected roadless areas. And while road building and logging provide jobs, the net value to the government of the national forest timber sale program is negative: a Government Accountability Office (GAO) study estimated that the Forest Service timber program cost American taxpayers more than $2 billion from 1992 to 1997 and continues to average a net loss of about $400 million a year.

Set this against the positive contributions that intact forests contribute to the economy and human well-being. In 2001, Douglas J. Kreiger, a PhD economist, did a survey for The Wilderness Society, a review of scores of studies that estimate the value of what economists call *ecosystem services* provided by the national forests. The numbers are quite stunning.

The studies that Kreiger reviewed vary considerably in their estimates, so he gave the range and then averaged the estimates. Here are a few findings.

One-fifth of the country, that is, about sixty million people, rely on water that comes from national forest watersheds. This is worth a bit more than $18 billion a year. Forests purify water and absorb particulate matter from the air. This is worth another $18-plus billion. Forests produce food—mushrooms, edible greens, medicinal plants, and, of course, animals that are hunted. That runs up to another $10-plus billion.

Carbon sequestration in these warming days is a hot topic, and trees are looked to more and more to help absorb our prodigious emissions of carbon from vehicles, power plants, and myriad other facilities. Dr. Kreiger's study found that the national forests contribute about $3.4 billion in carbon-sequestration services a year. This figure comes from Forest Service calculations that each ton of carbon removed from the atmosphere provides a benefit of $65. Roadless areas alone, by the Forest Service's figuring, provide about $1 billion in carbon sequestration services. Other contributions (biological diversity, soil formation, pest control—birds eat bugs for free, saving money otherwise spent on pesticides) add up to another $5 billion or $6 billion annually. The total is variously estimated as high as $64 billion a year. The Krieger study closely parallels a study commissioned by the Heritage Forests Campaign, conducted by John B. Loomis and Robert Richardson of Colorado State University.

The numbers only estimate the value of ecosystem services. Overall, the biggest number, not surprisingly, is for recreation. This number comes from the Forest Service, which estimates that recreational activities—camping, fishing, and hunting—on the forests pump $110 billion into the nation's economy each year. This counts all national forest areas, not only roadless areas, but roadless areas are worth far more for recreation and for the ecosystem services they provide than areas that have been roaded, logged, and drilled.

The value of roadless areas was investigated in a different way by Paul Lorah and Rob Southwick in a study undertaken for the Oregon Natural Resources Council and the World Wildlife Fund. They set out to investigate the assumption that withdrawing forests from the timber base imposed a net cost to the local economy in dollars and jobs. They studied trends in Oregon, and came up with some startling findings.

In general, they found that the fraction of the state's economy generated by resource-extraction activities was falling rapidly, down fully 50 percent since the 1950s, while "industries that benefit from the presence of environmental amenities are growing rapidly." They further stated, "Many economic sectors benefit from the presence of environmental amenities and protected areas. These sectors, such as tourism and retirement, are increasingly important sources of economic growth." Protecting land from logging and mining, in other words, is generally a net economic benefit. They concluded that

> this analysis shows that the presence of wilderness and Forest Service
> roadless areas are associated with economic growth. It does not prove
> that wilderness and roadless areas cause economic growth. It does,
> however, support the well-publicized idea that in the rural west, eco-
> nomic security is associated with counties that no longer rely on the
> environment as a source of raw materials for export, but instead use
> the environment as a magnet to attract tourism, retirees, and small
> businesses.

These studies are academic, but businesses understand this value first-hand. The purveyors of recreational equipment know full well that their customers value forests over clear-cuts, and the roadless controversy caused them to get themselves organized and spring into action.

The Outdoor Industry Association (OIA), with headquarters in Boulder, Colorado, has more than 1,200 members—L.L. Bean, Sierra Designs, North Face, Recreational Equipment Inc., river runners, and other recreation interests. The association printed postcards for their members to distribute in their stores. This was patterned after the campaign to get the federal government to impose strict standards for organic food. In that case, health food stores were recruited to be distribution points for postcards and other material.

Cards from customers and letters signed by hundreds of businesses urging support for the moratorium—and later for the Clinton administration's Roadless Area Conservation Rule—poured into the Forest Service. And the OIA helped put together the Forest Roads Working Group, a remarkably diverse collection of conservation and business interests that set to work with meetings and seminars that would eventually produce a document with strong support for keeping roadless areas roadless. The Working Group included the OIA, plus Wildlife Forever, the Wildlife Management Institute, The Wildlife Society, Trout Unlimited, the Izaak Walton League of America, the Pinchot Institute for Conservation, and even International Paper.

The OIA, with underwriting from the Pew Charitable Trusts (see chapter 5), published a report surveying what it called *The Active Outdoor Recreation Economy*, and estimated that, overall, these outdoor activities contribute $730 billion to the U.S. economy each year, of which $88 billion goes to the treasury in taxes. Outdoor recreation also provides an estimated six and a half million jobs.

The OIA, in a related episode, got into a well-publicized tussle with Utah's then governor Mike Leavitt (who later served as administrator of the Environmental Protection Agency and subsequently as secretary of the Department of Health and Human Services). Leavitt had signed a deal with then Secretary of the Interior Gale Norton that stripped protection from 300,000 acres of Wilderness Study Areas (WSAS) in Utah and eliminated the possibility of adding new study areas nationwide. WSAS are roadless areas that exist on lands managed by the Bureau of Land Management (BLM) and that have been proposed for permanent protection as wilderness. These WSAS tend not to have many trees on them, but they are important and beloved by hikers, campers, and others for many of the reasons that forested roadless areas are.

The OIA was so incensed by this deal that it threatened to take its annual trade show out of Salt Lake City, which would have cost the city millions. Leavitt met several times with leaders of the association, and eventually the governor promised to seek protection for all roadless areas five thousand acres or bigger and to oppose some oil and gas exploration proposals. The OIA agreed to keep its event in Salt Lake, at least until 2009.

The industry was getting organized. As Paul Gagner, of Gregory Mountain Products in California, told Jeff Barnard of the Associated Press (5-12-04), "What we are recognizing as an industry is that we need to have a concerted voice in politics. In the past we've had a fractured voice." It seems likely that outdoor industry people will remain strong allies of environmental groups, at least when it comes to protecting the public lands.

A different sort of outdoor industry—commercial fishermen and fishing guides—were strong supporters of the Clinton Roadless Area Conservation Rule as well, since damage to forested watersheds tends to damage spawning beds and therefore the fishermen's livelihood. As Harvey Young, who was a fishing guide in Idaho, put it in an interview conducted at his home in southern Oregon in 2007, "The streams coming out of the Selway-Bitterroot Wilderness are crystal clear, perfect for trout, because there are no clear-cuts, no roads." Young now works as a salmon and steelhead guide in southern Oregon and northern California and is an adamant supporter of keeping roads out of remaining roadless areas.

Looking through the other end of the telescope, Taxpayers for Common Sense, an organization that ferrets out government waste, fraud, and abuse, issued a report in 2002 that analyzed what it deems the squandering of taxpayers' money by the Forest Service, much of it on the road program. The report zeros in on the *purchaser road credit* (now called the *specified road credit*) program, which has the effect of masking the amount of subsidy provided the timber industry by the government.

Here's how it works: A timber company bids a sum for a timber sale, let's say $100,000. To get access to the trees, the company has to build $20,000 worth of roads. The $20,000 is deducted from the $100,000 bid for the timber, so the government gets only $80,000 for its trees. Cost overruns are borne by the government, as are the eventual costs of decommissioning the roads. The Taxpayers for Common Sense report concludes that "taxpayers have provided more than $116 million in direct subsidies to the timber industry for construction of logging roads at a cost of nearly $15,000 per mile."

Those numbers pale in comparison with the maintenance backlog of more than $10 billion mentioned in chapter 3, and the report notes that "despite an $8.4 billion backlog in road maintenance [the report came out in 2002; the number has risen steadily] and the almost 80 percent of national forest roads that do not meet basic roads standards, President Bush's FY 2003 budget request reduced annual road maintenance by $3.3 million and increased timber subsidies by $12 million."

The road maintenance liability seems straightforward enough, but Under Secretary of Agriculture Mark Rey, who oversees the Forest Service, has a different take from environmentalists, such as Mike Dombeck, and many others, as he does on so many things:

I think that's an argument that kind of misses the point. Yes, we have a backlog and we are dealing with it as we right-size the existing transportation system. And we are closing and decommissioning many more miles of roads than we're building. So we are in the process of right-sizing the existing transportation system. That having been said, that in my judgment is a question and an issue whose solution is separate and separable from the question of some of the areas that are now roadless. Are there reasons, values, resources that will need future access for good and appropriate purposes at some point at a future time? Should

we maintain flexibility to do that by whatever means financially is avail-
able? In some cases the access is paid for by the person who is seeking it.
In many of these roadless areas the primary value is their remoteness,
where the remoteness manifests itself in several other ecological values
that shouldn't be eliminated by making it more accessible.

To sum up, intact forests have economic benefits that are not always apparent and taken into account. Likewise, logging programs have costs that are
often masked and misunderstood.

But for some, economics is not the most important consideration one way
or the other. The religious community was approached by Suellen Lowry,
formerly a wildlife lobbyist for Earthjustice and a sister of Mike Lowry, a former governor of Washington. Lowry had left her position at Earthjustice and
moved with her husband to a small town in far northern California. Kevin
Kirchner, Lowry's former boss in Washington, DC, asked her to try to orga-
nize religious and scientific leaders to support the roadless effort that was
just then gaining steam. This, as with many other efforts, was underwritten by the Heritage Forests Campaign with money from the Pew Charitable
Trusts.

Lowry went on the faith circuit. She turned up at religious gatherings
across the country, asking pastors, rabbis, ministers, evangelicals, deacons,
priests—anyone identified as a leader of a religious community—to sign a
letter urging the Clinton administration to take bold steps to protect roadless
areas on the national forests. Lowry roamed through cafeterias at lunch-
time, buttonholing people as they waited in line, as they ate lunch, as they
left the room. She contracted with Peter Illyn of Restoring Eden to send sig-
nature gatherers to Christian rock concerts, which attract many thousands
of people. The signatures were not hard to gather. After all, a call to protect
God's creation resonates easily and deeply with people of faith.

In the end, Lowry and the others gathered signatures of more than two
thousand people on a letter that said, in part, the following:

As people of faith concerned with our responsibility toward God's mar-
velous creation, we would like to commend you for launching a process
to protect roadless areas in our national forests. We urge you to continue
this process by drafting a strong and effective policy that protects these pris-
tine regions fully. . . . We value these untouched forests not only for the

vital ecological functions they provide, but also because they so clearly reflect our Creator's handiwork. They reflect God's majesty, power, and beauty in a unique way, as do all of the amazing variety of creatures they shelter. Forests are like a temple constructed by God, where we can worship and draw close by marveling at God's endless wisdom and creativity. . . . The Scriptures make clear that protecting God's forests, and the many aspects of creation they embody and protect, is not merely sound policy but holy obligation. The Scriptures tell us that the earth does not belong to us, but to God, and that we are the tenants charged with its care. (1999)

Mark Jacobs, then the director of the Coalition on the Environment and Jewish Life, hand-delivered the letter to the religious-group liaison officer at the Clinton White House on June 29, 1999. Within twenty-four hours, John Podesta, the White House chief of staff, was on the telephone to Jacobs, inviting him to bring a delegation of religious leaders over for a chat. "As a lobbyist, it's very hard to tell which of all the things you do, the tools you use, actually produces the result you seek," Lowry said in a telephone interview in early 2008, "but not this time. That letter really got their attention."

Less successful was a letter sent to President Bush on April 30, 2001. This was a much less ambitious but arguably more urgent effort, signed by twenty leaders from Catholic, Protestant, and Jewish organizations. It was a stern letter urging the administration not to abandon the Roadless Rule:

As leaders and members of the U.S. faith community, we view caring for God's creation as an important moral and religious obligation. We also view protection of the environment as a responsibility shared by all. We urge you to exercise this responsibility by implementing the Roadless Area Conservation Policy immediately and by vigorously defending it in court.

Many members of the religious community played a significant role in urging development of this strong policy to protect the undeveloped areas of our national forests. We were there in hearings, letters, and prayers. We have rejoiced at the prospect of protecting 58.5 million acres of some of our nation's most pristine forests. . . .

In this season of celebration for many faith traditions, we are reaching out to you in hope. Let us together be humble in the face of God and

*God's creation. Let us protect the remnants of wild creation while we still
can, for the sake of our faith, our children, future generations, and God's
myriad creatures. The roadless policy gives us all a wonderful opportunity to join together to protect these critical wild areas. We hope and
pray that you will, on behalf of us all, take this opportunity fully. (2001)*

President George W. Bush did not answer.

Shootouts in Idaho and Wyoming   8

THE FIRST TWO LAWSUITS, filed in 2001, challenging the Roadless Area Conservation Rule were assigned to Judge Edward J. Lodge of the federal district court in Boise, who had been appointed to the bench by the first President Bush in 1989.

The Justice Department, acting as counsel for the Forest Service and nominally defending the agency and its rule, immediately started telegraphing that it would not mount a straightforward defense of the Roadless Rule. On February 20, 2001, Boise Cascade asked Judge Lodge to block the rule before May 12, when Secretary of Agriculture Ann Veneman had said it would go into effect.

The Justice Department replied by asking for more time to answer the motions, and promised that it would delay putting the Roadless Rule into effect until the judge could rule on them. Judge Lodge refused to give the federal defendants more time and asked for an answer by March 20.

On March 21, the administration filed its response. It urged the judge not to block the rule immediately, pointing out that it wouldn't go into effect until May 12, then reminded the court that it could always block it after that date: "Plaintiffs have not identified any irreparable harm which will befall them before May 12, 2001, the current effective date of the regulations," the brief argued:

> *Because the parties have not challenged the absence of harm during the period prior to the effective date of the regulation, the Court should be reassured that the status quo can be appropriately maintained and the parties will not suffer any irreparable harm . . . . In fact, the parties did not raise any arguments that harm will occur before May 12 because they cannot. The Rule does not become effective until that date and prior to the effective date the parties have their prior rights to challenge any agency conduct they find objectionable. Moreover, if the agency acts prior to May 12, and USDA reserves the right to do so, all parties will have opportunity to challenge that process and the court has complete discretion to prevent irreparable harm.*

The government went on to outline several options open to the court short of issuing an injunction, including issuing a stay of the effective date of the rule.

A defense of the rule, as promised by the new attorney general, this was not. Doug Honnold and Tim Preso, along with Pat Parenteau, speaking for the environmental-group intervenors, likewise argued against any injunction, stating that any delay of the Roadless Rule's taking effect could lead to timber sales that then would lead to irreparable harm to the national forests and to the interests of their clients.

Judge Lodge called a hearing on the various motions for March 30. Attorneys for the State of Idaho, the Kootenai tribe, Boise Cascade, and their coplaintiffs argued that the rule should be declared illegal immediately. They said that the rule was illegal and that their interests would be irreparably harmed without an immediate and nationwide injunction.

Then it was the turn of the Justice Department's lawyer, Andrea Berlowe, to present arguments for the Forest Service. This had been a very public and very controversial matter for a long time, as we have seen. The plaintiffs had submitted briefs and affidavits on a wide range of issues, both legal and otherwise. The environmental-group intervenors had as well. Now it was the government's turn to present its position. As it happened, Ms. Berlowe was up and down in the space of two or three minutes, having read her prepared remarks:

> *Good morning, Your Honor, and may it please the court, my name is Andrea Berlowe, I represent the United States in these cases. The United States Department of Agriculture's position on this motion*

[for a preliminary injunction] is that the Court should wait to rule until the new administration has had the opportunity for a full review of the roadless rule and can inform the Court of its position on the preliminary injunction motion . . . .

The review is a review of the promulgation process of the rule as well as the substance of the rule. The roadless rule is a significant policy shift involving nearly 60 million acres or approximately 30 percent of the National Forest system, a variety of national forests throughout the country, a voluminous administrative record, and well over 1 million public comments and 600 public meetings as the Court is aware. There are many serious issues involved in this review, and the new administration and the United States Department of Agriculture wish to give all the issues full and fair consideration . . . .

The United States has not yet taken a position on the merits of the claims of the State or of the other Plaintiffs because of the ongoing review process.

And that was it. No discussion of any of the many issues raised in the litigation before the court. As the Lieberman report (see chapter 6) had suggested, the administration probably had indeed "taken a position on the merits of the claims of the State or of the other plaintiffs" and was simply testing the breeze in Judge Lodge's courtroom before it adopted a final strategy.

Doug Honnold of Earthjustice, representing most of the environmental intervenors (Forest Service Employees for Environmental Ethics were represented by Scott Reed), argued that the Forest Service hadn't been legally required to do an environmental impact statement at all, since the Roadless Rule was protecting land, not harming it. He argued that an injunction was not appropriate since no harm to the State of Idaho was imminent. And he insisted that the Roadless Rule was perfectly legal and proper.

Andrea Berlowe had promised to submit a status review to the court by May 4. Judge Lodge agreed to wait until then before deciding on the injunction motions, though in an April 5 order denying the injunction he made his feelings plain: "The Court conclusively finds that the comment period was grossly inadequate and thus deprived the public of any meaningful dialogue or input into the process—an obvious violation of NEPA," the National Environmental Policy Act.

On May 4, the administration submitted its status report to the court. It was four pages long, little more than a white flag. It conceded that the plaintiffs had legitimate concerns:

> The USDA . . . acknowledges the need to include public participation in the forest planning process. States, Tribes, local communities and this Court have voiced significant concerns about the process through which the Rule was promulgated. After a review of the Rule and administrative record, the USDA shares many of these concerns. . . . It is critical, therefore, to ensure that Americans who live near these inventoried roadless areas have a sufficient and meaningful opportunity to comment upon the Rule's development and implementation.

Remember, please, that the Forest Service had held six hundred public hearings on the proposed rule, at least two in or adjacent to every single national forest in the system. How this failed the "sufficient and meaningful" test, the government declined to explain. And finally, the status report stated that "the USDA shares plaintiffs' concerns about the potential for irreparable harm in the long-term under the current Rule."

The status report went on to say that the injunction the plaintiffs were seeking was unnecessary because the department was working up amendments to the rule that would make Idaho and the rest of the challengers happy. The new proposed amendments would be announced and offered for comment the following June (2001), government lawyers assured the court. In other words, the government said it agreed that the rule was badly flawed and was taking steps to fix it.

The plaintiffs—Idaho, Boise Cascade, the Kootenai tribe, and others—shot back that the rule was clearly illegal and should be blocked immediately and permanently. Skeptics pointed out that the administration's promise to amend the rule may have been a veiled invitation to Judge Lodge to go ahead and issue an injunction. The intervenors, feeling ever more isolated, insisted that the rule was perfectly legal and that it should be left alone.

Mike Dombeck read the status report with dismay, but without much surprise. He was still chief of the Forest Service, since such political-appointee holdovers are allowed to keep their jobs for 120 days. The status report had been submitted in his name, but he hadn't been consulted, hadn't been shown a draft prior to its being submitted to the court, the first and only time such a thing happened. Dombeck remembers that "everything was quiet until I saw the answer to the Idaho suit. I knew it was all over." He mulled it over for a couple of weeks, then fired off a letter to Secretary Veneman on March 27. It was a lengthy and thoughtful meditation on the role and accomplishments of the Forest Service he had served so long, along with many sensible suggestions for the new secretary. "I hope," Dombeck wrote,

> the Administration's intent is not to negotiate a settlement with those opposed to roadless area protection. Doing so would undermine the most extensive multi-year environmental analysis in history. . . . Controversy over roadless areas has persisted for decades. I hope you will withstand political pressure and not reopen this divisive debate. . . .
>
> Most important, not a single private land owner or corporate interest would continue to build new roads in pristine areas while saddled with a crumbling 386,000 mile road system with an $8.4 billion road maintenance backlog liability. . . . It makes little sense to harvest old-growth forests simply to bring their short-term economic values to market. . . . The mark of a truly wealthy nation is not measured in acres harvested, rivers dammed, oil barrels filled, or mountaintops mined. Our maturity is most ably displayed by demonstrating mastery over ourselves.
>
> I recognize that short-term political imperatives run rampant in Washington, DC. Please remember that the decisions you make through your tenure will have implications that last many generations. You cannot fail if you allow your loyalty to the land and to those yet to be born to take precedence over all other organizational and political realities.

With that, Dombeck resigned, moved back to Wisconsin, and took up a teaching position at the University of Wisconsin at Stevens Point. His suggestions would be almost universally ignored.

Back in Idaho, Judge Lodge chose not to wait for the administration's revision of the rule, which proved to be prescient—the proposed new rule, promised for June 2001, wouldn't in fact appear until three years later. Judge Lodge declared the Roadless Rule illegal and issued a nationwide preliminary injunction, to remain in effect until a hearing could be held on the merits of the cases.

He found that the plaintiffs were likely to prevail in their case, which argued that, despite six hundred public meetings and well over a million and a half public comments, the rule violated provisions of the National Environmental Policy Act that require ample opportunity for the public to participate in such decisions. Judge Lodge also found that "the Roadless Rule poses serious risks to the National Forests and adjoining lands by restricting active management activities that have already been planned and precluding Forest Service officials from considering certain management techniques in planning future management activities." It was May 11, 2001.

The administration, which might have been expected to appeal the decision to the next higher court, as is customary, declined to do so. The intervenors' attorneys, now officially on their own, notified the Ninth Circuit Court of Appeals that they intended to contest Judge Lodge's order. It was an odd and very unusual situation. The defendants were walking away from a case; whether the court would permit the intervenors to pursue an appeal was an intriguing and vital question.

Allowing intervenors to appeal when the defendant drops out is unusual but not unprecedented. In a case decided in 1992, two Alaska Natives, an Aleut and a Tlingit, challenged a regulation issued by the U.S. Fish and Wildlife Service that forbade the use of sea otter pelts for clothing and handicrafts, with certain exceptions. The trial court found for the plaintiffs and against the government. Friends of the Sea Otter, a private, nonprofit group, had intervened on the side of the government defendants to support the regulation. At first the government appealed (the Friends group also appealed), but then changed its mind, dismissed its appeal, and agreed to abide by the lower court's ruling. Friends of the Sea Otter argued that it should have the right to pursue the case to defend the regulations. The appeals court agreed, and the Friends carried the appeal to its conclusion.

They lost. The regulations were upheld, but the principle that an intervenor may in some circumstances independently pursue an appeal was affirmed.

A second case supported the first. In the early 1990s, the Idaho Farm Bureau sued the U.S. Fish and Wildlife Service (which is one of the most frequently sued federal agencies) for granting Endangered Species Act protection to the Bruneau hot springs snail, a tiny mollusk whose range is confined to a five-mile strip of thermal springs along the Bruneau River and Hot Creek in Idaho. The Idaho Conservation League and the Committee for Idaho's High Desert intervened on the side of the government to defend the listing.

The trial court found against the government, saying that the listing was "arbitrary and capricious," which is a violation of the Administrative Procedure Act.

The federal defendants did not appeal the trial court's ruling, but the intervenors did. Again, the court (both these cases took place in the Ninth Circuit) ruled that the intervenors had the right to prosecute their appeal. This time the intervenors won. The district court was overruled.

In other federal circuits intervenors have been refused when attempting to appeal a decision when the named defendant has declined to appeal. The Supreme Court has not yet considered this situation.

The same general proposition can work in favor of groups that intervene on behalf of a plaintiff. In a case finally decided in the spring of 2007, the U.S. Environmental Protection Agency (EPA) sued Duke Energy for violations of the Clean Air Act. The Environmental Defense Fund (EDF), a private nonprofit group, intervened on the side of the government. The appeals court ruled against the government and in favor of Duke Energy, and the EPA decided to fold its tent. EDF, however, petitioned the Supreme Court to review the case, and to nearly everyone's surprise the high court agreed—and found unanimously against Duke.

Within a week of receiving the environmentalists' motion on the Roadless Rule, the Ninth Circuit agreed to allow an expedited appeal to proceed. The plaintiffs could, and would, argue that the intervenors should not be allowed to pursue the case on appeal, but the Ninth Circuit agreed at least to listen to arguments to the contrary.

On July 10, as a preliminary step in rewriting or replacing the rule, the Forest Service asked the public to submit comments on ten questions that could have been written by opponents of the rule—as, in a way, they were. They were of the kind pollsters ask when they already know the answer they want to hear. The rejoinders in italics are taken from an analysis prepared by Earthjustice.

- What is the appropriate role of local forest planning as required by NFMA [the National Forest Management Act] in evaluating protection and management of inventoried roadless areas?
  You may notice that this speaks only of "local" forest planning, not regional or national.

- What is the best way for the Forest Service to work with the variety of States, tribes, local communities, other organizations, and individuals in a collaborative manner to ensure that concerns about roadless values are heard and addressed through a fair and open process?

  Same bias. No mention of the national interest in the national forests.

- How should inventoried roadless areas be managed to provide for healthy forests including protection from severe wildfires and the buildup of hazardous fuels as well as to provide for the detection and prevention of insect and disease outbreaks?

  "Healthy forests" is code for opening roadless and other areas to logging under the guise of post-fire salvage, hazardous fuels thinning, or insect control.

- How should communities and private property near inventoried roadless areas be protected from the risks associated with natural events, such as major wildfire that may occur on adjacent federal lands?

  Again, focus only on nearby communities and property owners.

- What is the best way to implement the laws that ensure States, tribes, organizations, and private citizens have reasonable access to property they own within inventoried roadless areas?

  More of the same, and such access was provided for in the original Roadless Rule.

- What are the characteristics, environmental values, social and economic considerations, and other factors the Forest Service should consider as it evaluates inventoried roadless areas?

  No problems here.

- Are there specific activities that should be expressly prohibited or expressly allowed for inventoried roadless areas through Forest Plan revisions or amendments?

  This is a tricky one. There was one overriding activity expressly prohibited by the original rule: road building. This question assumes that management will be carried out through the forest plan process, which is what led to the chaos that led to the Roadless Rule in the first place.

- Should inventoried roadless areas selected for future roadless protection through the local forest plan revision process be proposed

to Congress for wilderness designation, or should they be maintained under a specific designation for roadless area management
under the forest plan?
*This question may have been designed to get antiwilderness forces
riled up; hard to say. Many inventoried roadless areas would not
qualify for wilderness designation, so this seems a bit of a red herring.*

- How can the Forest Service work effectively with individuals and
groups with strongly competing views, values, and beliefs in evaluating and managing public lands and resources, recognizing that
the agency cannot meet all of the desires of all of the parties?
*This whole exercise seems to be an abdication of responsibility. Of
course the agency can't please everybody. The previous rule sought to
do what was right as well as what the public, in overwhelming numbers, said it wanted.*

The idea, it seemed quite clear to the environmental groups, was to solicit
support for a drastic revision of the Roadless Rule that might, in the view of
people of outgoing Forest Service chief Mike Dombeck's persuasion, actually
make things worse than the status quo, since existing protections of some
roadless areas in some forests would be swept away.

The environmental community swung back into action, asking people
to renew their support for protecting roadless areas. This effort generated
another 800,000 comments, most of them urging retention of the rule as
written.

By this time only three of the legal challenges were moving forward. The
Ninth Circuit had Judge Lodge's injunction to consider. The Alaska and
Wyoming cases were being briefed and Wyoming's would soon be argued.
All the others save the two in North Dakota, where negotiations were under-
way toward a possible settlement, were put on hold pending the outcome of
the rest.

The Dakota cases were in fact quite different from the others. There, the
land managed by the Forest Service consists of three national grasslands,
where there is little or no logging and wild creatures compete with livestock for forage. The two suits filed in the state against the Roadless Rule
argued that it was in conflict with a state law that says that section lines—
the lines on a map that divide land into square miles—are state highways,
even if there's nothing there, and that the state can claim a right-of-way and

construct roads along those lines whenever it wants to. Here's how Mark Rey, under secretary of agriculture, explains the situation:

> In North Dakota there was a peculiarity wherein the state asserts through state law the right to build roads along section lines so that section lines are bona fide easements that private land owners are obligated to recognize should the state want to execute them.
>
> All of our grasslands acreage in North Dakota, and these are grasslands not forests, are reverted lands—they were privately held, unsuccessful dryland agriculture experiments that reverted back to the federal government in the 1920s and '30s under the Bankhead Jones tenant farmer act.
>
> The state of North Dakota held that the federal government is to some considerable degree bound by the terms of the deeds that reverted lands were covered by and that the federal government is no different from any other private landowner in North Dakota therefore.
>
> In that case the state was primed to litigate to preserve its prerogative to basically build roads, as necessary for state transportation. And there again we thought that letting that case litigate out wasn't necessarily going to be in our best interest because the state might have prevailed at the district court level, and the district court in North Dakota might give a fairly generous reading of what the state's rights really are in this case, and that it might be better to see what rights of way the state really was concerned about. So we effectuated a settlement agreement there with [an] environmental intervenors' agreement that creates a road reconciliation process that allows the state to come forward and sort of prove up its existing roads.

Todd True of Earthjustice, who had intervened in the two suits on behalf of several environmental organizations, sees it a bit differently. Yes, the Forest Service worked out a deal with North Dakota and the four objecting counties, but without participation of the intervenors. The intervenors didn't much like the settlement agreement and filed formal objections with the court. The court delayed the settlement and directed the parties to see if they could find a compromise, and eventually they did and agreed to dismiss the cases, leaving the door open to further litigation if subsequent actions threatened to sacrifice the grasslands to too many miles of roads. True insists that the suits could have been beaten—and that they might yet arise and be litigated. He thinks Mark Rey's legal analysis is questionable.

Next to come was the argument over the appeal of the Idaho injunction at the Ninth Circuit, which was held in October 2001, in Seattle. The judges were curious as to the whereabouts of the defendants. (The U.S. attorney for the region was actually in the rear of the courtroom but didn't identify himself.) Doug Honnold of Earthjustice, who represented the main body of environmental intervenors, and Pat Parenteau of the Vermont Law School, who represented Forest Service Employees for Environmental Ethics in the companion case, explained that the defendants had abandoned the case and that the intervenors were therefore representing the rule and the public's interest in it.

Legally, there were two threshold questions that the appeals court had to address. One, had Judge Lodge acted properly in allowing the organizations to intervene in the first place? And two, were the intervenors entitled to pursue the case once the government had dropped out? Doug Honnold argued that yes was the correct answer to both. And there were the merits of the case to consider as well; for example, was the rule legally adopted?

The three-judge panel consisted of Andrew J. Kleinfeld, a conservative; Warren J. Ferguson, a liberal; and Ronald M. Gould, a centrist. Kleinfeld immediately questioned Honnold closely on what he considered the intervenors' lack of standing. The judge referred to an opinion he had written recently that dismissed a case brought by the Sierra Club for lack of standing. He argued that only the federal government can defend cases brought under the National Environmental Policy Act. And he suggested that Judge Lodge had erred in granting intervention to the environmental groups. Judge Kleinfeld's questioning went on so long that Honnold's time was used up. Judge Ferguson asked Judge Kleinfeld to allow Honnold a few minutes to discuss the merits of the case. Judge Kleinfeld reluctantly agreed.

Pat Parenteau credits Judge Gould with getting around Judge Kleinfeld's objection to the groups' intervention, pointing out that the intervention was "permissive" rather than "as of right," which means it's within the trial-court judge's discretion to allow such groups into a case like this one.

The three judges thanked the lawyers (of whom there were officially sixteen representing the various interests, not including the Department of Justice) and withdrew to consider their decision. It took them almost fourteen months to announce their conclusion.

The panel split two to one. The majority, comprising Judge Gould and Judge Ferguson, ruled for the conservationists, upholding their right to carry the appeal in the absence of the federal defendants. "In fact," Judge Gould wrote for the majority, "the government declined to defend fully from the outset, suggesting that the government itself saw problems and wanted to amend the Roadless Rule. Under these circumstances it is clear, as the court itself recognized, that the presence of intervenors would assist the court in its orderly procedures leading to the resolution of this case, which impacted large and varied interests." Furthermore, the judges ruled that the plaintiffs' case was shaky at best and unlikely to succeed at trial. They lifted the injunction and sent the case back to Judge Lodge to consider the merits. The Roadless Area Conservation Rule was in force for the first time. The case in Judge Lodge's court would lie idle for years.

In his dissent, Judge Andrew J. Kleinfeld argued that the intervenors should never have been allowed into the case in the first place, let alone allowed to take the place of the defendants on appeal. "Essentially, the majority holds that as long as a would-be intervenor asserts a defense that is 'responsive' to the claims against the proper party defendant, intervention is proper," Judge Kleinfeld wrote. "The majority's position would allow intervention by virtually anyone who has some affected interest.... Such a result is absurd...."

Judge Kleinfeld also insisted that Judge Lodge was correct in issuing the injunction, that the Forest Service had been illegally hasty in pushing the rule through to conclusion. Telegraphing his stance, he wrote that "national forests... are not 'natural environments.' They've been a managed rather than a natural environment for a hundred years. For most of that time they were managed to serve as a federal tree farm...." Judge Kleinfeld may not have done so deliberately, but he echoed complaints conservation groups had been making for years about the way the forests had been managed. The point here, however, was that nearly a third of the system had survived intact, had been spared such management. "What we have here," the judge concluded, "is a case where the agency attempted a massive management change for two percent of the nation's land on the eve of an election and shoved it through...."

The losing side—Idaho, the Kootenai tribe, Boise Cascade, and the others —asked for what's known as a rehearing *en banc*. In most circuits this means assembling all the appellate judges to rehear the case; the Ninth Circuit has so many judges (twenty-seven active, another twenty-two on senior status) that an *en banc* hearing involves just eleven judges, always including the chief judge. The request for an *en banc* hearing was denied. The circuit had spoken clearly. The Roadless Rule was legal and the injunction must be dissolved.

In Wyoming, meanwhile, in Judge Brimmer's courtroom, matters took a different and peculiar turn.

The complaint filed by the plaintiffs largely paralleled the case in Judge Lodge's court in Idaho, but it added a new twist. And the government's approach to defending the rule was dramatically at odds with the stance it had taken in the Idaho court.

The twist was an accusation that the White House, the Department of Agriculture, and the Forest Service under Mike Dombeck had illegally conspired with the environmental groups to write the rule and deliberately leave the timber industry, the states, the counties, some tribes, and other interested parties out of the process in violation of the Federal Advisory Committee Act. (This allegation had been offered months before in the premature challenge filed in Idaho before the rule became final; that case had been dismissed and never considered.)

A report prepared by the Republican staff of the congressional Subcommittee on Forests and Forest Health of the Committee on Resources early in 2000 had outlined the accusations that Wyoming would later take into federal court:

> *On October 28, 1999, the Committee on Resources requested documents from the Forest Service and the White House concerning the President's initiative to restrict use on 40 to 60 million acres of "roadless areas" on the National Forests. Staff has to date received, and conducted a preliminary review of, thousands of pages of documents provided by the Administration.*
>
> *A preliminary review of these documents reveals that the Administration's decision was made improperly, in apparent violation of the due process rights of affected parties, as well as applicable statutes enacted by Congress to protect those rights, such as the Administrative Procedure Act and the Federal Advisory Committee Act.*
>
> *Information received in response to the document request indicates that the Administration's roadless area initiative was developed in an*

environmental vacuum—with virtually all input coming from a select few in the environmentalist community . . . .

These individuals had continuous communication with and access to the Federal employees that were directly involved in the creation of the rule-making.

Lawyers for the State of Wyoming and the other plaintiffs asked the court to order the intervenors and the defendants to turn over membership lists, financial records, private correspondence, both electronic and conventional, and other material, and they asked for permission to interview representatives of the groups and their attorneys under oath, seeking to prove that there had been collusion.

The environmental groups dismissed the requests as simple harassment and an attempt to win the case by drowning their opponents in motions and procedural skirmishes and also violate privacy and attorney-client privilege. Ken Rait of the Heritage Forests Campaign declared in answer to his subpoena as follows:

The strategic communications between myself and advocacy allies, during the development of the Roadless Area Conservation Rule, are not mere matters of history. Those past communications are directly relevant to our current communications and inform and guide our on-going exercise of our First Amendment rights to petition the government as well as our role in the continuing public debate over how our undeveloped national forest areas should be managed . . . . The intrusive nature of these discovery requests is unprecedented and in no uncertain terms chills my capacity to do the public interest advocacy work I have done for the last fourteen years.

Harriet Hageman, who made an appearance earlier in this narrative in Judge Brimmer's courtroom (see chapter 2), at this time represented the State of Wyoming. She issued subpoenas to Rait and many of his colleagues seeking to question them about their activities.

Jim Angell, of Earthjustice's Denver office, had to devote nearly full time for a year and more to contesting the requests for documents, organizing the ones they would agree to turn over, and preparing his clients for their depositions.

Angell filed for a *protective order* from the court to shield his clients from what they considered a fishing expedition. Judge Brimmer's magistrate, Judge Beaman, granted part of the order and denied part, mainly to protect financial information and the identities of members of the various plaintiff groups. The defendant-intervenors were ordered to produce reams of "redacted" documents, copies with sensitive, privileged information blacked out. Rait's subpoena was quashed.

Ironically, this came at about the same time many of the same organizations were complaining that a task force appointed by Vice President Cheney to recommend elements of a new energy policy had consisted solely of industry representatives and had met as an ad hoc advisory committee illegally and in secret.

The Justice Department, meanwhile, for reasons it declined to explain and continues to decline to explain, took a dramatic change of course. Whereas in Idaho it had all but conceded that the Roadless Rule was illegal, in Wyoming (and, earlier, in briefs submitted in North Dakota) it conceded no such thing: "Wyoming's claims should not prevail for a variety of reasons," it argued to the court. "The Forest Service complied with all applicable laws and acted well within the broad discretion conferred upon it by Congress to manage National Forest System lands." It even cited the recent decision by the Ninth Circuit finding the law valid and Judge Lodge's injunction mistaken. It argued that the plaintiffs had no right even to bring the case for a variety of reasons and that they should immediately be shown the door.

It was a curious turn of events for which the government offered no explanation, insisting that it continued to support "roadless values," without explaining what that meant.

Agriculture Under Secretary Mark Rey, for his part, insists there was no change in policy or approach:

Our position was that we were going to retain the 2001 rule but replace it with a rule that we thought would do a better job of balancing state and local interests while still protecting roadless area values. That's what we said before any of the litigation reached pleading stage in May of 2001.

So our position then going into the Idaho and Wyoming litigation— those were the only two cases where actual pleading occurred—was basically to tell the court that we thought the 2001 rule was not legally infirm but that we were probably going to make some adjustments to it.

In both cases the courts disagreed and said they thought the rule
was legally infirm. In those cases we elected to not appeal because we
were pretty far down the road in writing our own rule, which we thought
would be a better result.

Reading between the lines, it seems likely that one or both of two explanations is the case. For one thing, the government may have decided that it would be easier to amend the existing rule than to start over with a whole new rule, which meant defending the old rule in court and revising it later, as the government had told Judge Lodge in Idaho it would do. Starting from scratch would involve a new environmental study, hearings, public comments, and would take many months. In an interview, Mark Rey was stopped by his counsel from answering a question about this since litigation concerning the question was still ongoing.

The other conjecture, voiced by some of the people close to this extended drama, was that the rank-and-file attorneys in the Department of Justice were prepared to mount a forceful defense of the rule, but in Idaho, in any case, they were overruled by political appointees.

Either way, when it came to Wyoming, it didn't make any difference why or even whether the government had changed its tune. Judge Brimmer was not going to be swayed by the rule's defenders whether they be the federal government, the environmental lawyers, or both. He found the rule illegal, not only within Wyoming, where his court had jurisdiction, but throughout the rest of the national forest system as well. He did not speak to the question of whether the intervenors had illegally colluded with Clinton administration officials in violation of the Federal Advisory Committee Act.

His reasoning differed a little from Judge Lodge's. He agreed that the process by which the rule came into being left things to be desired, but what persuaded him was the argument that the Forest Service was summarily trying to set aside 58.5 million acres of wilderness, when only Congress has that power under the Wilderness Act of 1964. "The Forest Service, through the promulgation of the Roadless Rule, designated 58.5 million acres of National Forest land as a de facto wilderness area in violation of the Wilderness Act," he wrote, even though there are many activities permitted in roadless areas that are forbidden in wilderness areas.

Shortly after Judge Brimmer's decision was released, two organizations based in Washington, DC, Community Rights Counsel and Citizens for

Responsibility and Ethics in Washington, charged that Judge Brimmer held as much as $1.1 million worth of investments in oil, gas, and mining companies that were in a position to benefit if the Roadless Rule were eliminated. The groups argued that Judge Brimmer should have disqualified himself from the proceedings and asked the Tenth Circuit in Denver to investigate.

Brimmer was defiant and unapologetic: "My financial holdings include certain gas and oil companies. None was a party to *Wyoming vs. United States Department of Agriculture*. I also own some small mineral interests and am not aware of any that are located within a national forest. During the more than two years this matter has been pending in my court, there have been thousands of pages of documents filed and numerous hearings conducted. The parties in this case have never raised any issue about the propriety of my involvement." Brimmer said that any of the parties to the case could file a motion raising the issue, either in his court or in the Tenth Circuit. None did, and the matter faded away.

Doug Honnold of Earthjustice had argued the case before Judge Brimmer, filling in at the last minute for an ailing Jim Angell. By the time the injunction appeared, Angell was back in action and promptly sent formal notice to the Tenth Circuit that his clients wished to ask that court to review Judge Brimmer's decision, which he said was clearly mistaken on its own merits and at odds with the recent decision by the appeals court in the Idaho case. The administration, having argued forcefully in favor of the rule in the Wyoming court, did not file an appeal. Clearly they had abandoned the strategy of saving the rule so they could amend it.

So now there was the curious situation where a Wyoming judge had declared the rule illegal and banished it from the entire country side by side with a ruling from an appeals court that declared the rule valid and in effect. If the Tenth Circuit refused to hear the appeal by the environmental groups, or if it sustained Judge Brimmer's decision, there would be what is called in the profession *a split in the circuits*, which frequently means a case is on its way to the Supreme Court.

Two months after Judge Brimmer's decision was announced, the Justice Department let pass its deadline for filing an appeal. Two months after that, the same agency submitted a friend-of-the-court brief to the Tenth Circuit Court of Appeals urging it to deny the environmental groups' motion to take an appeal of the case. "When the Executive, upon due deliberation in its decision-making processes, determines to end litigation over a discretionary regulatory policy, a private party does not have standing to use the judiciary to override that legal/policy determination," the Justice Department argued. The agency pointed out that Wyoming had objected to the intervenors' being allowed to get into the case. Further, they wrote that

> the USFS was not legally compelled to promulgate the Roadless Rule, or to retain it. In these circumstances, the intervenors cannot demonstrate an injury sufficient to establish Article III standing to pursue further litigation when the Executive has determined on behalf of the United States not to do so. The decision of the Ninth Circuit to let intervenors carry an appeal in the Idaho roadless case ignored the most relevant Supreme Court decision.

Another curious situation. The administration had walked away from a case it lost but might well have won on appeal, then asked the appeals court to drop the case as well, effectively switching sides and joining the plaintiffs. The Tenth Circuit announced that Angell was free to file his opening brief—it would decide later whether the groups actually qualified to pursue the appeal.

The Tenth Circuit would wait a year and a half before scheduling oral argument, which was eventually held on May 5, 2005.

The Biological Value of Roadless Areas 9

SHE LOOKS IN THROUGH the breakers to the foaming waters of the big river. It is time. She dives to miss the turbulence and knifes through the current into the strangely bland fresh water of the river. The attraction is irresistible.

She is a king salmon, a chinook, now four years old, three feet long, weighing nearly thirty pounds. She has swum countless thousands of miles in the Pacific, foraging for sardines and anchovies and the tiny shrimp known as krill. Now, she is determined to return to the stream where her parents had performed the ageless ritual that she is about to reenact.

To get to her goal is a daunting challenge. Once she breasts the breakers, she must swim eight hundred miles up the Columbia and Snake and Salmon and Clearwater and Selway rivers. On the Columbia she must pass the Bonneville Dam, then The Dalles Dam (which drowned the magnificent Celilo Falls), then John Day, then McNary. Next, on the lower Snake River, await Ice Harbor, Lower Monumental, Little Goose, and Lower Granite dams. All are outfitted with what humans euphemistically call *fish ladders*: steep man-made canals with crossbars where a fish can pause and catch a breath, as it were, which is the only way to get past the massive dams.

The reservoirs behind the dams are huge and stagnant, their temperatures uncomfortably—even dangerously—warm. These four Snake River dams have been at the heart of heated legal and political struggles for years, with scientists and environmentalists arguing that removing or breaching them is the best, maybe the only, way to restore once-mighty salmon populations to the Columbia Basin. Agricultural interests, which ship grain and other crops on barges down the river via the reservoirs and their locks, fight fiercely to keep the dams intact. The government argues that the dams are a natural feature of the river now, just like boulders and eddies. Some of the consumers of the modest amount of electricity generated by the dams resist breaching suggestions as well, fearing that their bills will rise.

Yet the chinook thrashes onward, never stopping to eat, driven by forces as old as time. Once she has run the gauntlet of dams, with a final exhausted dash up the roiling cascades known as Selway Falls, she has only to find her destination. Finally, smelling or otherwise sensing home, she veers right out of the Selway River into Meadow Creek, knowing somehow that this is her ultimate goal in life.

She meanders a few miles upstream, finds a spot to her liking, and waits for the future father of her young to appear. She has been swimming, with little rest and no food, for at least two weeks, covering nearly a thousand miles. Once a male chinook turns up, she will carve a shallow pit, a redd, in the gravelly bottom of the creek and deposit her eggs. The male will immediately fertilize the eggs with a spurt of semen—milt—then cover the eggs with gravel with a few flips of his tail. Both adults will soon perish. A few weeks later baby salmon, called *fry*, will begin to fight their way out of the gravel bed, starting the cycle once again.

The chinook's stroke of luck is that the stream she calls home is still a hospitable place to aim for. No reservoir covers its spawning beds. No silt or mud from hillsides damaged by roads or logging or mining or livestock grazing has ruined the stream, a fate that has befallen so many streams throughout salmon country and everywhere else.

Meadow Creek has survived to welcome its salmon precisely because there is no development nearby, and there is no development nearby because there are no roads in the watershed.

Another feature of Meadow Creek that makes it valuable biologically is that, even though it's nearly a thousand miles from the sea, it's less than two thousand feet above sea level. Most national forest wildernesses are high-elevation areas that don't contain much valuable timber. And given the elevation, they are less diverse and productive biologically than lower-elevation forests. The Forest Service was quite aware of this fact in its review of roadless areas in the 1990s and its eventual decision to protect them all. References to biological value are peppered through the environmental impact statement (EIS) prepared as part of the Roadless Area Conservation Rule process. The agency identified 220 species that live in roadless areas that are either legally endangered, threatened, or candidates for protection in one category or the other, and 1,930 others classified as *sensitive*. James Morton Turner in addresses these issues in *Conservation Biology*:

> Based on [the Forest Service's] scientific estimation, roadless-area con-
> servation would confer substantial benefits for most identified species by
> reducing the threat of habitat modification, protecting biological strong-
> holds, protecting areas devoid of invasive species, and complementing
> existing state and federal plans for endangered species recovery. Species
> that would benefit included wide-ranging carnivores to narrow endemic
> mollusks and plants. . . .
>
>   Based on its scientific assessment of the roadless areas and public
> support for conserving roadless areas, the Forest Service recommended
> prohibiting road construction on all [58.5 million acres of] roadless
> areas in 2000 (with some exceptions in case of emergencies, federal high-
> way construction or improvement, small-scale stewardship logging, or
> specific legal obligations). In explaining its final recommendation . . . the
> agency emphasized the ecological benefits of roadless-area conservation:
> "These areas provide a bulwark against the spread of non-native invasive
> plant species, support a diversity of habitats for native plant and animal
> species, conserve biological diversity, and provide opportunities for study,
> research, and education."

A study by James Strittholt and Dominick DellaSala, also published in *Conservation Biology*, bore out the proposition that roadless areas tend at least in some places to be biologically richer than wilderness areas. In studying the Klamath-Siskiyou ecoregion in northern California and southern Oregon, they found that roadless areas contained nearly four times more of what they call "heritage elements" *(1745)* than wildernesses, heritage elements being plants and animals of special conservation interests, including protected species.

As an ancillary observation, a preliminary study in the Clearwater National Forest in Idaho suggests what seems obvious: once-roaded areas can be restored to roadlessness by the decommissioning of roads to the benefit of wildlife and general biological health. There, the decommissioning of some six hundred miles of roads has led to a surge in the populations of elk, deer, and mountain lions.

A raft of scientists was organized by Suellen Lowry, who had organized the religious leaders as discussed in chapter 7, again under contract with Heritage Forests. On May 1, 2001, 291 scientists working in natural resource-related disciplines, including biology, forest ecology, geology, aquatic ecology, fisheries, soil science, and natural resource management, sent a letter to President Bush:

> We write to urge you to take decisive action to protect the remain-
> ing undeveloped and roadless areas within the national forests of the
> United States.... We are greatly concerned about the continuing loss
> and fragmentation of the nation's forests. In light of the many important
> benefits they provide, we feel it wise that the few remaining, intact road-
> less areas within the national forests be preserved. The final Roadless
> Area Conservation Rule, issued January 12, 2001, is an important step
> towards preserving the invaluable ecological services and the tremendous
> aesthetic and recreational benefits that intact forests provide.
>
> Scientific research has amply documented the greater health and
> resiliency of intact forest ecosystems versus those disturbed by roads and
> logging. Undisturbed forests are less susceptible to tree diseases, insect
> attacks, and invasions from non-native species, and are less likely to
> have suffered the adverse effects of fire suppression. These healthier eco-
> systems are in turn more able to withstand the effects of global climate
> change and act as refugia for sensitive wildlife and plant species, many of
> which are vulnerable to extirpation in more developed areas. Thus, intact
> forests can serve as reservoirs as surrounding landscapes become geneti-
> cally impoverished.

As with the pleas from religious leaders, the president did not answer. The last point in their letter is worth reinforcement here. There is little question that as global climate change begins to exercise its influence over virtually all living things on the planet, natural reservoirs including roadless areas will become ever more essential as refuges for wildlife of all kinds. And once civilization comes to grips with human-caused climate disruption and eventually reverses it, it will be from roadless areas, wilderness areas, national parks, wildlife refuges, and similar reserves that remnant populations of hundreds of species may be able to begin to reclaim their historic habitat and restore a natural balance, something like what we are losing so quickly today.

Skullduggery in Alaska 10

MEANWHILE, the legal case against the Roadless Area Conservation Rule in Alaska veered off the path followed by the Idaho and Wyoming cases. The state had filed suit not so much to attack the rule itself, but rather to get the Tongass National Forest, the largest in the system at nearly seventeen million acres, removed from the terms of the Roadless Rule. The other suits sought to invalidate the rule nationwide; Alaska's concerned only the Tongass. Logging had declined dramatically on the Tongass with the closure of large pulp mills at Ketchikan and Sitka, but state officials dreamed of a resurgence in the industry. Alaskan officials, particularly the congressional delegation of Senators Ted Stevens, Frank Murkowski, and Representative Don Young, also resented being told by the federal government how to manage what they considered really ought to be their land. One can easily imagine a movement arising in Alaska to renounce statehood and become an independent country.

In any event, the State of Alaska and the Forest Service saw what was going on in Idaho and Wyoming and they came up with a different approach for Alaska. Attorneys Eric Jorgensen and Tom Waldo of Earthjustice had been given the green light to intervene in the Alaska suit on behalf of the Southeast Alaska Conservation Council, the Sitka Conservation Society, the Alaska Center for the Environment, The Wilderness Society, and the National Audubon Society. While they waited for a briefing schedule, however, they learned that the State of Alaska and the federal defendants had reached an agreement in secret, without the knowledge of the intervenors (who were theoretically full parties to the case), an agreement whereby the Forest Service would issue within sixty days a proposed temporary regulation that would exempt the Tongass National Forest from the Roadless Rule until any formal amendments to the overall rule were completed. The agency also agreed to publish formal notice that it would exempt both the Tongass and the Chugach National Forest from the rule.

The Alaska case, in fact, was quite different from the others. Its core claim was that the Roadless Rule violated a provision of the Alaska National Interest Lands Conservation Act (ANILCA) of 1980, a law that created a number of protected areas in Alaska and expanded others. Buried deep in the statute is this statement:

> *No future executive branch action which withdraws more than five thousand acres, in the aggregate, of public lands within the State of Alaska shall be effective except by compliance with this subsection. To the extent authorized by existing law, the President or the Secretary may withdraw public lands in the State of Alaska exceeding five thousand acres in the aggregate, which withdrawal shall not become effective until notice is provided in the* Federal Register *and to both Houses of Congress. Such withdrawal shall terminate unless Congress passes a joint resolution of approval within one year after the notice of such withdrawal has been submitted to Congress. No further studies of Federal lands in the State of Alaska for the single purpose of considering the establishment of a conservation system unit, national recreation area, national conservation areas or for related or similar purposes shall be conducted unless authorized by this Act or further Act of Congress. (Sec. 1326 a, b)*

Alaska argued that the Roadless Rule was a withdrawal of land from the timber base and therefore illegal under ANILCA.

Agriculture Under Secretary Mark Rey, in an interview, explained his view of the situation:

> *The difference in Alaska . . . was that there are specific issues of law unique to Alaska . . . that we weren't that eager to have adjudicated because we*

*thought that there was some greater vulnerability there. In Alaska it was
the meaning of the "no more" clause in ANILCA and whether the 2001 roadless rule was a violation of that. The exact meaning of that clause has never
been adjudicated and there was, we thought, a pretty good chance that if
it was adjudicated in the case brought by the state of Alaska against the
federal government that we would get an adverse ruling out of the district court in Alaska. Certainly we could have appealed that but it's hard to
know where exactly that would end up. Our basic feeling was that we had a
pretty good chance of losing at the district court level, maybe a pretty good
chance of winning on appeal, but because the plaintiff in this case was the
state that was asserting a very deeply felt state right that had been secured
in legislation affecting that state uniquely that the state would probably
seek* certiorari *[ask for Supreme Court review]. We also felt that there was a
pretty good chance that if the district court opined on the meaning of the "no
more" clause, that that opinion could call into question any number of previous administrative set-asides made by either the Department of Agriculture
or the Interior in managing their lands in Alaska from 1980 to present, so
the prospect was not losing just the 2001 roadless rule but several administrative designations made in the land-management plans that the respective
agencies had used to manage their holdings from 1980 to present. Or from
the passage of ANILCA when Congress set aside all the new national parks
and wildlife refuges and monuments and wildernesses and said, at least in
the view of the state of Alaska, that there will thereafter be no more set-
asides done administratively by federal agencies. So that's why, in that case,
we were not interested in seeing it go to trial and affected a settlement with
the state of Alaska.*

Tom Waldo of Earthjustice, who had represented the environmental groups
that had been granted intervention in the case but frozen out of settlement
discussions, disagrees: "The state's 'no more' clause argument was a weak
claim at best and could easily have been defended in court. We had intervened in the case on behalf of several conservation groups and were fully
prepared to defend the claims, but Mr. Rey settled the case without consulting us. No wonder. The settlement gave the state and the timber industry
everything they wanted. The real reason for settling the case was to reopen
Alaska's national forest roadless areas to clear-cutting and roads." Despite

the demise of the Roadless Rule via this backroom settlement, the attorneys were able to block roadless-area timber sales through sale-by-sale challenges.

Environmental lawyers, led this time by Niel Lawrence of the Natural Resources Defense Council, said that Rey's logic was flawed. No new land was being protected or withdrawn. Existing wild lands were simply being preserved. It might have made for interesting legal argumentation, but that was not to be.

Then lawyers for the state and the Forest Service returned to court and told the judge they had reached agreement and would like to dismiss the case. The settlement was not lodged with or approved by the court, so there was nothing for the intervenors to appeal. Lawrence, Jorgensen, and Waldo searched vainly for a legal hook they could use to take the settlement to the appeals court for review but were unable to find one. Six months later, in the slow period two days before Christmas in 2003, the Forest Service announced formally that the Roadless Rule, no matter what might happen elsewhere, no longer applied on the Tongass National Forest. The technique of settling lawsuits quietly and keeping the public from participating in the negotiations had become a hallmark of the Bush administration, being used again and again in a variety of cases in many places.

Hunters and Anglers
Get Riled Up

11

As we discussed in chapter 7, the amount of money spent on backcountry recreation in the United States each year is substantial: $730 billion by the estimate of the Outdoor Industry Association (OIA). So it was not surprising that OIA's many hundreds of member organizations would rise to defend the Roadless Area Conservation Rule. Nor was it surprising that the people who fuel the outdoor recreation industry—hunters and anglers in particular—would get involved as well. And they are numerous: the U.S. Fish and Wildlife Service estimated that in 2001 more than 82 million Americans hunted, fished, and watched wildlife, spending well over $100 million in the process. And, there were political implications in the growing interest among hunters and anglers in the roadless debate. Hunters and anglers, particularly hunters, for many years have tended to be Republican, distrustful of government, uneasy with regulations, afraid their firearms might one day be confiscated. The struggle over the Roadless Rule would begin to change that.

One example among many is an outfit known as the Backcountry Hunters and Anglers of Eagle Point, Oregon. A flier they produced is typical of efforts mounted by similar groups across the country:

Our freedom to hunt and fish depends on habitat. "Roadless areas" are large backcountry areas on public land, largely free of roads and accessed

99

by trail. These areas contain priceless and irreplaceable resources for hunters and anglers. It's no coincidence that states with the most road-less areas—Alaska, Idaho, Montana—also have the strongest hunting and angling traditions.

These backcountry lands offer unmatched habitat security, a rare and shrinking feature crucial for popular big game species such as elk, mule deer, bighorn sheep, mountain lion, mountain goat and bear. These areas tend to have the healthiest, most robust herds and grow the most mature bulls, bucks and rams. In general, roadless lands support the longest hunting seasons and most liberal hunting regulations. Biologists at the Montana Department of Fish, Wildlife and Parks, for example, say the state could not maintain its five-week-long general hunting season with-out the habitat security provided by roadless areas.

Roadless areas are important sources of clean water and fish habi-tat. They are generally the healthiest spawning and nursery habitat for ocean-run salmon and steelhead and the strongholds of native fish such as bull, redband rainbow and cutthroat trout. Clean, cold water flowing from high roadless areas feeds downstream fisheries for native and non-native trout alike.

Biology aside, roadless areas provide important social benefits such as peace and quiet, and solitude that we greatly value. Backcountry Hunters and Anglers want roadless areas to stay as they are—so our children and grandchildren can enjoy the fine hunting and fishing we ourselves have grown up with. Given the massive road maintenance backlog on our national forests, it is only common sense to repair our current road net-work before building new roads into valuable habitat.

A coupon was attached to the flier, inviting people to join the organization ($25 for an individual, $35 for a family).

One other organization that went all out in defense of the Roadless Rule was the Theodore Roosevelt Conservation Partnership (TRCP), which rallied hunters and anglers to "Take Action Now" via their web site. Their argu-ments closely paralleled those of the Backcountry Hunters and Anglers:

Why are Inventoried Roadless Areas important to hunters and anglers? Roadless areas generally provide large contiguous blocks of the best hab-itat for big game species like mule deer, elk, moose, bighorn sheep and

mountain goats, and the least degraded streams and lakes where trout,
salmon and other desirable fish species dependent on clean water, stable
stream flows and consistent lake storage can thrive.

The absence of roads prevents fragmentation of secure habitat that
big game species need for population survival. Roadless areas in large
blocks also reduce the vulnerability of both fish and wildlife species to
excessive harassment and harvest and allow populations to thrive at
levels supporting longer hunting seasons and easy-to-purchase tags.
(www.trcp.org/ch_roadless.aspx)

The partnership then encouraged hunters and anglers to add their names to the effort to save roadless areas "so TRCP can make sure your voice is heard in discussions determining the fate of inventoried roadless areas in your state."

Ken Rait of Heritage Forests would later observe, "I cannot underscore strongly enough the importance of the partnership's survey that found the vast majority of hunters and anglers in support of roadless area protection. I heard from various folks in the White House that these findings substantially increased the administration's comfort zone with moving forward on the roadless initiative."

Even the National Rifle Association, long a staunch opponent of federal land-use regulation, began to feel heat from within its own ranks, from hunters dismayed at the rapid loss of game habitat to oil and gas development in particular. Ronald L. Schmeits, a second vice president of the association, was quoted by Blaine Harden of the *Washington Post* as saying, "The Bush administration has placed more emphasis on oil and gas than access rights for hunters. We find that our members are having a harder time finding access to public land" (1-7-07).

"It's a no-brainer," said Hal Herring, a contributing editor for *Field and Stream* magazine in the same *Post* story. "The NRA stance [opposing] the roadless rule is a mistake. There are no more roadless areas being produced."

It's not possible to know exactly what the extent of the influence of the hunters and anglers in the debate over the Roadless Rule was, but it was clear that the Bush administration was becoming concerned as the 2004 presidential and congressional elections approached. Many administration officials were dispatched to assure anglers and hunters, particularly in western red states, that the administration was a strong supporter of their favored activities.

A New Rule
Is Proposed　12

BUT WHAT OF THE PROMISE made to Judge Lodge that the Forest Service would rewrite the rule to accommodate the objections of the various states, industry groups, counties, and a few tribes that felt shortchanged by the Roadless Area Conservation Rule? In an *Advance Notice of Proposed Rulemaking*, issued in June 2002 (see www.roadless.fs.fed.us), the Department of Agriculture (USDA) had floated the idea of adding a provision to the rule that would allow governors to opt out of the rule, but it was not clear whether that was something the department was considering seriously. A year and a half dragged by. Mark Rey had a meeting with the conservation group representatives in Washington, DC, in January 2004, as the coming election campaign began to dominate the news. He said they were working on a new rule, but that if nothing had been announced by May, one could safely assume there would be no announcement before the November election.

May passed without any news. In mid-June, a bill in the House of Representatives to cut off all funding for road building in the Tongass National Forest was approved, to the surprise of many, and was sent to the Senate. Then, on June 28, 2004, a little-noticed paragraph titled "Agriculture Department" appeared in the *Federal Register*:

> *Due to the continued legal uncertainty of providing protection for road-*
> *less areas through the application of the roadless rule, the agency is*
> *proposing to amend the roadless rule by replacing the prohibitions of*
> *the January 2001 rule with a procedural rule that would set out an*
> *administrative process for State Governors to petition the Secretary of*
> *Agriculture to establish or adjust management direction for roadless*
> *areas within their State. Such petitions would be evaluated and, if agreed*
> *to, addressed by the Secretary in subsequent rulemaking on a State-by-*
> *State basis. (vol. 69: 37240)*

Note the use of the word *amend.* This will prove critical as the litigation progresses.

It may well have been a trial balloon, to gauge how strong the reaction would be. Marty Hayden of Earthjustice thinks it may have been a way to force the hand of the Office of Management and Budget, which, he had heard, had been holding Mark Rey back from releasing the new rule. Chris Wood, a former deputy to Forest Service chief Mike Dombeck who went from the Forest Service to Trout Unlimited, speculated that the lack of reaction to the June 28 announcement led Rey and others to conclude that the public was no longer so passionately interested in the Roadless Rule and had moved on to other concerns.

Whether or not that was the case, on July 12, 2004, with the conventions looming (Senator Kerry had locked up the Democratic Party's presidential nomination by this time, and had been a staunch supporter of the Roadless Rule since its inception), Agriculture Secretary Ann Veneman announced that the Bush administration had a new Roadless Rule to offer the nation. It would preserve "roadless values." It would involve local communities in management decisions. And it would add a new and unprecedented twist to the system as telegraphed in the June 28 notice: Governors would be given eighteen months to file petitions with the Forest Service to preserve roadless areas in their states. Or, in the alternative, they could petition to have roadless areas opened to roading and subsequent logging, mining, and other kinds of development. The Forest Service would then have six months to consider the petitions, but it would not be obliged to approve them. Petitions filed after the end of the eighteen-month deadline could be considered as part of the agency's regular petitioning process under the Administrative

Procedure Act. The administration, it seemed clear, had finally decided to abandon the Clinton-era rule altogether and start again, from scratch.

Environmentalists immediately denounced the new rule, loudly and colorfully. Marty Hayden of Earthjustice told *Greenwire*, "You could have a real hodge-podge of requests coming out of the states resulting in national forests that don't look very national" (7-13-04). Craig Gherke of The Wilderness Society said, "You don't have state Social Security plans. Why should we have state roadless plans?" (*San Diego Union Tribune*, 7-13-04). Phil Clapp of the National Environmental Trust said the rule change would be "the single biggest giveaway to the timber industry in the history of the national forests" (*Rocky Mountain News*, 7-13-04). Jane Goodall and E.O. Wilson joined 125 of their scientific colleagues in opposing the rule change. And Doug Honnold added, "The state governors can request more logging and more road building and more oil and gas development and more hard-rock mines than we've ever had before in these areas. If your goal is to maximize the amount of corporate development of our national forests, this is a great plan. If your goal is to protect clean drinking water and wildlife, it's an awful plan" (*Los Angeles Times*, 7-13-04). Marty Hayden was quoted again, in the *New York Times*: "This doesn't ensure that a single acre of roadless area gets protected. Everything could be up for grabs" (7-12-04). Everything, in this case, Hayden pointed out, would include roadless areas that had been protected under individual forest management plans before the Roadless Rule had been dreamed up in the first place.

Even Bill Clinton, three and a half years out of office, weighed in, in the *Los Angeles Times*: "Governors would be required to petition the Forest Service to keep certain forests roadless—ignoring the stark political reality that few governors are likely to stand up to the pressure of timber companies and other special interests to protect national forests in their states" (8-14-04).

And other newspapers across the land weighed in as well, nearly all of them critical. "The Bush administration has taken apart so many environmental regulations that one more rollback should not surprise us," editorialized the *New York Times*:

Even so, it boggles the mind that the White House should choose an election year to dismantle one of the most important and popular land preservation initiatives of the last 30 years—a Clinton administration

rule that placed 58.5 million acres of the national forests off limits to
new road building and development.

There are no compelling reasons to repudiate that rule and no obvious
beneficiaries besides a few disgruntled Western governors and the tim-
ber, oil, and gas interests that have long regarded the national forests as
profit centers. (7-18-04)

The *Washington Post* was sarcastic:

"Veneman Acts to Conserve Roadless Areas in National Forests." So
read the Orwellian headline on the Agriculture Department's announce-
ment Monday about Secretary Ann M. Veneman's move to junk a Clinton
administration rule that protected nearly 60 million acres of national
forest from road-building, logging and other development. But no one
should buy the Bush administration's effort to give this anti-environmental
action a green spin: It had pledged to uphold the roadless measure, but
its proposal would instead eviscerate protections for some of the
country's last unspoiled wilderness. (7-16-04)

The *Louisville Courier-Journal* painted a bigger picture; "This administration favors states rights—except in the cases of corporate liability, utility
regulation, marriage, medicinal marijuana, physician-assisted suicide and
anything else it thinks states might get wrong. There is still hope. Congress,
which must fund road construction in national forests, could refuse to do
so" (7-15-04).

The *Lexington Herald-Leader* added, "As a final insult, the public gets to
pick up the tab for damaging its own forests, since the roads are federally
funded" (7-15-04).

A rare voice supporting the Bush administration, the *Rocky Mountain
News* editorialized as follows:

Too many people today feel that any attempt to correct the top-down
imbalance in the way federal lands have been managed amounts to an
attempted giveaway of resources—as if state officials and local residents
have no interest in maintaining the natural assets that surround them.
No one expects the volume of timber harvested on federal lands to return

to what it was 20 years ago. But since as much as 40 percent of the forests designated roadless in 2001 bears a significant risk of catastrophic fire, it's hardly unreasonable to keep careful timber harvesting as an option for improving forest health. (7-15-04)

Mike Dombeck, the former Forest Service chief, ruefully declared the new rule "brilliant." It takes the heat off the Forest Service, he explained, and puts it directly on the governors. And in the West, where 97 percent of the roadless areas are, the timber industry has considerable influence over statehouses. In one glaring exception, Governor Bill Richardson of New Mexico announced that he would petition for all the roadless areas in his state to remain that way if the rule were changed as outlined. Arnold Schwarzenegger, the governor of California, who, though a Republican, would break often with the Bush administration, likewise suggested that he might take steps to protect roadless areas in his state. Others pointed out that some of the states most profoundly affected by the rule change could be key in the upcoming election (no matter what the *Times* may have said), namely Oregon, Colorado, and a few others.

Secretary Veneman's announcement set a deadline of September 15, 2004, for comments to be received, and again partisans on all sides urged their supporters to rev up their computers.

If the administration had thought roadlessness was no longer of interest to the public, it was mistaken. So many comments were submitted that the deadline was extended for two months, until after the election. There was speculation that the administration was surprised at the depth and breadth of opposition to the proposed new rule and decided to let it macerate until after election, but that's only conjecture. In any event, the election came and went. George W. Bush won a second term. And the administration proved to be in no hurry to go final with its new rule, preoccupied as it was with Social Security and Iraq. By the deadline, another 1.8 million comments had been logged; 97 percent opposed the new Bush rule.

But what weight do such numbers carry? The environmental side spent vast quantities of time, effort, and money gathering signatures and comments in an attempt to influence the agency, to convince it that the public was solidly on the side of protecting roadless areas. Did it work? Here's Agriculture Under Secretary Mark Rey:

My view is that the point of a public notice and comment rulemaking is to collect public comment and insights from people that are affected by an agency proposal. The more detailed and specific the insights the more useful they are in deciding how to craft the rule to reflect some of what you hear. Now, that all having been said, it is a time-honored tradition to rally the troops to see how many comments you can generate in favor or in opposition to a proposition. Those comments typically aren't very detailed. They're in the nature of "we support this" or "we oppose that," "please do this" or "please don't do that."

They're instructive in two respects. One, they can show the breadth of concern, and two, they can also show how well organized the proponents or the opponents of a particular proposition are. But I don't think any Executive Branch agency looks at a notice-and-comment rulemaking process as the equivalent of a referendum or a ballot initiative. So therefore we don't typically count votes for the sake of counting votes.

And in the case of the Roadless Rule there was a very well-organized effort with a lot of funding behind it. If you look at the IRS Forms 990 of the organizations that were primarily involved in the effort—at one point we did, just out of curiosity—and we totaled somewhere in the neighborhood of fifteen million dollars of foundation money that was devoted to this initiative. If you look at it that way, two million comments isn't all that impressive. That's about seven bucks a postcard or email.

That was a time, in the 1990s, when donor foundations in this area of philanthropy were very much into funding initiatives, whether they were ballot initiatives or other initiatives to effectuate a particular outcome. And people who were seeking donations from those foundations were putting together campaigns. "This is a campaign we're going to mount if you're willing to fund it. Here's what it will look like."

That doesn't mean that the comments are less worthy, but it does mean, to me at least, that you can't say this is a spontaneous reflection of a public upwelling of views. Because it's an organized campaign. A well-organized campaign.

Well, I guess the way I look at it is that this is a representative democracy and when it's important to count votes, and just count votes, is when we're electing our representatives, and beyond that we've sort of tasked them with the responsibility of listening to what we say, keeping that in mind but not necessarily acting because x number of us have

weighed in in favor of a proposition and x number of us have weighed in
against a proposition. Now, if too often they keep moving in the direc-
tion that's supported by the smaller number of people, then we take our
responsibility as citizens and vote them out of office. I look at that as
where it's most important to count votes. It's important to listen, to
register the concern, but not to decide that you're going to do something
one way versus another by virtue of the fact that x number of people
recommended one course of action that was more than recommended
an alternative course of action.

An important fact that Rey neglected to mention, and that the environmental groups are quick to point out, is that officials in the Forest Service and
the other agencies are not elected, never have to run for office. They certainly
listen intently to members of Congress, but they are largely insulated from
the electoral process, and therefore not directly accountable to the public.

The Tenth Circuit Court of Appeals scheduled oral argument on the appeal
of Judge Brimmer's injunction for May 4, 2005. As the date approached, anon-
ymous sources in the USDA told reporters and environmentalists that the
agency was hurrying to get the new governor-petition rule ready for release,
maybe on the same day as the hearing. This would give Wyoming's lawyers
the opportunity to suggest that the judges adjourn the hearing and dismiss
the lawsuit because the law being litigated had been replaced. May 4 dawned
with no announcement, so the hearing went forward. Jim Angell of Earthjustice,
speaking for the intervening conservation groups, said that Judge Brimmer's
claim that there hadn't been adequate opportunity for public comment was
preposterous: "This regulation was the subject of more public involvement
than any other in the nation's history. If this doesn't pass muster, nothing
ever will" (Associated Press story carried in the *Denver Post*, the *Billings
Gazette*, and other newspapers, 5-5-05).

Jennifer Golden, the assistant state attorney for Wyoming, argued that
the case should be dismissed because the intervenors had no right to appeal
the case and that Judge Brimmer's injunction meant the rule no longer existed.
"It does if we reverse him," appeals Judge Michael McConnell said. The
judges ended the argument session without indicating how they might rule,
or when, or even whether.

Sure enough, the very next day, Mike Johanns, the former Nebraska governor who had replaced Ann Veneman as agriculture secretary in early 2005,

announced what had been anticipated for months—the administration was replacing the Roadless Area Conservation Rule with a new rule that would invite governors to submit petitions recommending how they would like to see roadless areas in their states managed. He also invited people to apply for positions on a new advisory committee, which would review the petitions as they were submitted and make recommendations on their disposition. The committee, he suggested, would include representatives of all groups with interest and expertise in the management of national forest roadless areas.

Whereas the Clinton administration had produced an exhaustive environmental impact statement on the original rule, the Bush administration did no new environmental documentation to go with its new rule. Officials had solicited public comment through the U.S. Postal Service and via email but had held no public hearings. The *Federal Register* notice announcing the new rule explained that it was essentially the *no-action* alternative considered in both the draft and final environmental impact statements for the 2001 rule, so therefore no new environmental analysis was required. Furthermore, the new rule was exempt from any requirement to do new environmental analysis, since it was "designated for categorical exclusion. Categorical exclusions . . ." the notice explained, "avoid unnecessary documentation of minor environmental effects in environmental assessments and allow agencies to focus their environmental review effort on the major actions that will have a significant effect on the environment. . . . " (vol. 70: 25654). Categorical exclusions generally mean that the Forest Service is not required to conduct an environmental study every time it wants to paint an outhouse or repave a parking lot. In this case, the agency was arguing that lifting protection from some fifty million acres of national forest land fell under the same exclusion.

A brief filed later by the states of California, Oregon, New Mexico, and Washington stated the following:

> *In rescinding the Roadless Rule, the Forest Service makes the startling claim that even if an EIS [environmental impact statement] is required, the Roadless EIS suffices: the agency is merely adopting the document's "no action" alternative. However, the "Purpose and Need Statement" in the Roadless Rule FEIS [final environmental impact statement], which explained and justified both a prohibition on development of roadless areas and the achievement of this objective through a nationwide rule,*

cannot, as a matter of logic or law, explain and justify a Roadless Repeal
rule that implicitly reaches the opposite policy conclusion. Likewise,
where the entire supporting Roadless Rule FEIS explains why the no-
action alternative does not achieve the agency's "Purpose and Need," the
Forest Service cannot rationally conclude, absent a new analysis, that
this alternative should be adopted.

The states went on to observe that the 2000 final environmental impact
statement (FEIS) had nothing to say about a petition process or any alternatives to such a process: "The Petition Process was nowhere predicted,
described, or analyzed in the 2000 FEIS—that is, it was not among the 'alternatives' presented in that document—making the FEIS facially incomplete
as a description and analysis of the agency's new 'Proposed action.'"

The environmental groups' lawyers immediately began to review the new
rule—which would go into effect sixty days later, on or about Independence
Day, 2005, to see if it could be attacked in court. The lack of an environmental study seemed to offer some promise, and the repeal and replacement
might also be vulnerable under the Administrative Procedure Act or the
Endangered Species Act.

Historical Digression

Natural Resources and Local Control

13

DURING THE Ronald Reagan administration (1981–89), wheels had been set in motion to undo federalism in favor of more state and local control of the public lands and the resources on and under them. Reagan's interior secretary, James Watt, favored handing control over public resources to local jurisdictions and private interests. The extreme manifestation of this was a movement that called itself the Sagebrush Rebellion, which favored "returning" federal lands to the states, even though those lands had always been in federal ownership. Watt proclaimed himself not a sagebrush rebel, then proposed draconian measures to appease the rebels. Watt tried, in fact, without success, to make the Wilderness Act (1964) expire after twenty years.

The management of public lands and other conservation issues had been largely nonpartisan until the Reagan administration took office in 1981. Richard Nixon had signed the National Environmental Policy Act in 1970, quickly followed by the Clean Air Act (1970), the Clean Water Act (1972), the Endangered Species Act (1973), and several other seminal statutes. Gerald Ford signed the National Forest Management Act in 1976. Environmental matters did not become highly politicized until the advent of the Reagan administration, and even that was not the result of Reagan's folksy conservatism. His approach to environmental matters as governor of California had been primarily laissez-faire, nothing remotely like the attack his administration mounted on environmental laws and institutions when it took over the White House and the executive agencies.

When he was governor of California, Reagan had tapped Norman "Ike" Livermore, a former board member of the Sierra Club, as his secretary of resources. Livermore reportedly persuaded Reagan to oppose a proposed new trans-Sierra Nevada highway and a huge reservoir on the northern coast of California.

By the time Reagan became president, however, his agenda was controlled by far-right ideologues and business titans. James Watt, Anne Gorsuch Burford of the Environmental Protection Agency, and others, however, were too outspoken for their own good. Their rhetoric was so incendiary that the public rose up in righteous anger, and most of their "reforms" were stopped cold. Watt, it was often observed, even by himself, was the best fund-raiser the environmental movement ever had. Watt finally had to go in 1983 when, in a speech to the U.S. Chamber of Commerce, he described an advisory panel he had appointed as composed of "a black, a woman, two Jews, and a cripple." The quote was carried in nearly every newspaper in the country on September 21, 1983. He resigned on October 11.

The George W. Bush administration proved to be something else again: quiet, stealthy, clever, determined, and unwavering. Opposition to the Roadless Area Conservation Rule fits perfectly with a philosophy that mistrusts government, especially the federal government. In the end, doing away with the rule by itself wasn't enough. Giving symbolic control—or, if not control, at least the opportunity for major influence—to the state governors, who would might be heavily influenced by industry, as Bill Clinton pointed out, is perfectly logical for these revolutionaries.

Agriculture Under Secretary Mark Rey, chief architect of the 2005 petitions rule, justified it this way:

There have been three times in the time period since 1964 when the people who occupy the chair I sit in, and who thought themselves substantially smarter than I believe myself to be, thought that it would be a grand idea to try to resolve the issue in one fell swoop through a nationwide rulemaking.

The first of those efforts was conducted in the Nixon administration in the late 1960s, an effort that was called the Roadless Area Review and Evaluation, subsequently known as RARE I. And, as all the data from all the forests were assembled, it quickly became apparent to the people who were doing it that the database wasn't very good. It certainly wasn't very uniform and aggregating it and trying to deal with it through a single rulemaking was not going to be a very successful endeavor. So RARE I didn't make it to the final rule stage.

The second time it was tried was in the Carter administration in the late 1970s, and that effort was called RARE II, not surprisingly. That effort did make it through the final rulemaking process, a very contro-versial outcome that was immediately litigated by a number of parties including several states. It was overturned because of lack of specificity by district court judge, now Supreme Court Justice Kennedy, as the result of a suit brought by the state of Califorina under then-governor Jerry Brown, and others.

Of course the third time, not yet proving to be the charm, was the Clinton 2001 roadless rule. In between those efforts the primary mech-anism for trying to resolve this was on a forest-by-forest basis and you could probably say that that wasn't entirely successful either because it wasn't resolved yet. The mere existence of the 2001 rule is fairly strong evidence that that approach was unsatisfactory to a large number of people.

So, if you look at that history, the lesson we took from it is that these are intensely political issues because they're basic resource allocation issues, but they're also heavily data-driven because you're talking about a large number of areas with site-specific peculiarities to them. You've got to know what's there and what's not, where the roads are and where they're not, what the condition, status, and situation is for each of these areas individually to do justice to them as you're trying to decide what their disposition should be.

So on the one hand you have an intensely political issue and an intensely data-driven issue. If you do a nationwide rulemaking you can get all the political closure you want. You can have the President of the United States stand on a ridgetop in Virginia and say "this is the final government decision" and that's what you're going to get. However, the agency hasn't been able to make that kind of decision worthy of a court's review, to stand up in the face of a court's review because the courts have always been able to look at it and say "that's not very site-specific, it seems arbitrary."

On the other hand, if you do it on a forest-by-forest basis you can delve deep into the individual details of each specific area and run each of those details to ground, so to speak, so that your decision hangs together from a substantive standpoint very well. Obviously that decision in that case comes from a forest supervisor, who is a GS-14 or GS-15 career civil servant, and that person isn't going to bring political closure to that decision because whoever is dissatisfied with the decision well knows there's a way to move it up the chain.

So looking at that history, we kind of said, what if we tried to break this into pieces that are digestible in a technical sense but still involve a large enough universe to bring some political closure? What if we did it on a state-by-state basis? With the state as a partner? With the governor, who is, after all, the one person who's elected to represent every person in the state, standing side-by-side with the agency and saying we think this is the best path. Probably we can get political closure. And if you do the job well, you probably can array enough facts and details that a court won't throw it out as being insufficient in terms of the quality of the record. So that's how we hit on this as a third path that nobody had previously chosen. (Mark Rey, pers. comm.)

This analysis, of course, is completely at odds with the view held by most in the environmental community. Marty Hayden of Earthjustice argues that it was exactly this forest-by-forest approach to timber management that led to the overcutting of the forest, which in turn led to the mutiny by the public that resulted in the original Roadless Rule.

Steve Kallick of the Pew Charitable Trusts agrees with this observation; his version is that the forest-by-forest approach led to a "balkanization" of the environmental community and hampered efforts to have national forest wilderness areas created and roadless areas otherwise protected across the country. Both would argue that that is precisely what Mark Rey and leaders in the timber industry would actually prefer.

The New Rule Is Challenged 14

On June 28, 2004, less than a month after the announcement of the Bush administration's new Roadless Area Conservation Rule, Kristen Boyles, an Earthjustice attorney in Seattle, sent a letter to the Forest Service alerting the agency to the fact that the new rule appeared to violate the Endangered Species Act, since the service had not consulted with the U.S. Fish and Wildlife Service (USFWS) and the National Marine Fisheries Service (NMFS), as required by law. Such consultations are meant to ensure that protected species will not be harmed by the imposition of a major new federal rule and therefore the *action agency*, the Forest Service in this case, must consult with these scientific agencies, which employ biologists and other scientists who can assess potential impact on protected species.

The choice of Kristen Boyles was strategic. She, along with Tim Preso and Tom Waldo, would file an expected challenge to the Bush rule in federal court in San Francisco—in the Ninth Circuit, in other words, which had already upheld the Clinton Roadless Rule in the case that began in Judge Lodge's Idaho court. The Endangered Species Act allegation was just the beginning— others would be added later. Before litigation under the Endangered Species Act (and several other federal statutes), the unhappy party (plaintiff) must give the government sixty days to rectify the alleged violation of law. This entails a letter that notifies the offending agency that it has two months to correct its transgression or it will face a lawsuit. Sixty-day notice letters rarely result in the action sought by the plaintiff organizations.

Meanwhile, the Tenth Circuit panel in Denver, noting the repeal of the Clinton rule and its replacement by the new Bush rule, dismissed as moot the case it had heard argued in May, at the urging of the State of Wyoming. At the request of Jim Angell, the lawyer who had argued that the Wyoming decision should be reversed, the court agreed to order Judge Brimmer to vacate his earlier order. Thus, it could not be cited in future skirmishes. As reported in earlier chapters, this would prove to be a pivotal event.

On July 12, 2005, the Bush Roadless Rule became final. It invited governors to submit petitions suggesting management strategies for roadless areas within their states. The petitions were to be submitted within eighteen months, whereupon the federal government would have six months to respond. The Forest Service, meanwhile, would be advised by a panel of experts from various fields.

The panel was dubbed the Roadless Area Conservation National Advisory Committee (RACNAC). The panel of thirteen was appointed in the fall by Under Secretary of Agriculture Mark Rey. It would analyze the governors' petitions and make recommendations to Secretary Rey about whether to accept, reject, or modify the petitions.

So the saga was now proceeding on two quite different paths: in the courts, with efforts to persuade judges to reinstate the original rule and dismiss the Bush substitute on one hand, and on the other, with the challenges to the Clinton rule still pending here and there, and in various statehouses, where governors first had to decide whether to work up petitions at all, and then go about doing so if they chose to.

Supporters of the Clinton Roadless Rule tended to assume that the petition idea came from Mark Rey, but Rey tells a different story:

> I think [the petition idea] came in part from the public comments we received on the advance notice of proposed rulemaking, in part from discussion with various states, and in part from discussions that we had internally. Additionally a consortium of interested groups—the Forest Roads Working Group—sponsored a third-party dialog during the period of time between the advance notice of proposed rulemaking and when we decided on our course of action. [The working group, as discussed briefly in chapter 7, was a coalition of interest groups on all sides of the roadless

debate, including a paper company and scientific and environmental
organizations.] So some of what went into the proposed rule was influ-
enced by the dialog at the Forest Roads Working Group. For instance,
the idea of a national advisory committee to advise the secretary on state
petitions was something that the Forest Roads Working Group proposed
in a slightly different context. (Mark Rey, pers. comm.)

A slightly different context indeed. What the working group recommended
was an advisory panel to advise the Forest Service on implementation of the
Clinton Roadless Rule, which it favored. And favored strongly. It said nothing about any state petition process because none had been put in place by
the time of the group's report, on March 26, 2003. The petition rule and the
advisory committee would not come into existence for two long years.

The Bush rule, no matter its provenance, was politically clever. It put the
prorule forces in a bit of a quandary. Some of them immediately denounced
the rule as a violation of the whole idea of federally owned forests ("Taking
the 'National' out of the 'National Forests,'" they thundered), and pledged to
fight it to the death in court. But meanwhile, should they participate in the
petitioning process and encourage governors to file petitions seeking to protect roadless areas? And why participate in the petition process if they were
trying to get the courts to throw out the rule that created it? On the other
hand, if the decision was to boycott the petition process, wouldn't that leave
the field open to prologging, antiroadless forces? Various groups came to
different conclusions.

Some national groups, including the Natural Resources Defense Council
and the Sierra Club, initially took the position that they would have nothing to do with the new Roadless Rule and the state-petition process, that it
was the Clinton rule or nothing. The Earthjustice lawyers told the groups the
new rule was illegal but, given the unpredictability of litigation, it wouldn't
be a bad idea to encourage governors to file petitions seeking protection for
the forests in their states in case the legal challenge to the new rule failed.
A large meeting was called by the Heritage Forests Campaign and held at
the headquarters of The Wilderness Society in Washington, DC. Eventually
a consensus was hammered out—the group would encourage and support petitions that called for 100 percent protection of roadless areas in
the given state. Accordingly, scores, if not hundreds, of local, regional, and
national groups, including many Sierra Club chapters, began putting heat

on governors to file strong petitions. Mat Jacobson of the Heritage Forests Campaign set out on a second, three-month road trip, reconnecting with the activists he had met a half-dozen years before. The agenda this time was how to bring pressure on governors to petition for total protection for all roadless areas in their states. Enthusiasm remained sky-high.

Meanwhile, the organizations that sought to challenge the legality of the Bush rule (referred to by them as the *Roadless Repeal* in the upcoming court battle) were slightly nervous at the possibility that their litigation would succeed, the petition process would be thrown out, and they would seen by some as spoilers, undermining the work of the grassroots activists involved in the petitions.

Relief came in the form of a lawsuit filed in August 2005 by Bill Lockyer, attorney general of California, Governor Ted Kulongoski of Oregon, and Governor Bill Richardson of New Mexico, who sought to have the Bush petition rule declared illegal. The State of Washington later joined as a plaintiff. Attorneys general of Montana and Maine submitted friend-of-the-court briefs in support of the four plaintiff states.

The states' lawsuit sought to apply a catch-22 to the administration's maneuvering. The National Environmental Policy Act requires preparation of an environmental impact statement (EIS) for federal actions that would have a major impact on the environment. The states observed that the administration had prepared no such statement to justify its substitute Roadless Rule, specifically that "the Roadless Repeal required a public analysis of the alternatives to, and environmental impacts of, repealing the Roadless Rule and creating a substitute 'Petition Process' for determining the fate of inventoried roadless areas." It did not provide any analysis at all.

The government argued that the EIS prepared as part of the original Roadless Rule process was adequate because it involved the same lands. But the states pointed out that the administration had previously agreed with the plaintiffs in the Idaho cases, which argued that the original EIS was inadequate and, further, that the original rule no longer existed. And, furthermore, the original EIS had justified the original Roadless Rule, not the proposed replacement rule.

The government responded that it would do environmental studies if and when any timber sales or oil and gas leases were proposed in inventoried roadless areas. The states replied that this was wholly inadequate because it wouldn't address the key question of whether one nationwide rule's replacement with another nationwide rule would have significant environmental ramifications and what alternative schemes might be considered and analyzed.

In addition, the National Environmental Policy Act requires an agency to explain in its environmental analysis the "purpose and need" to which the agency is responding in proposing alternatives. The original Roadless Rule obviously had nothing to say about its repeal and replacement with the petitions rule, and the new Roadless Rule was therefore illegal on that score as well, the states said.

Furthermore, the process the administration used to repeal the 2001 rule appeared to be in violation of the Administrative Procedure Act (APA), which, in the simplest of terms, requires government agencies to provide rational bases for their actions, and explain how the proposed actions jibe with other pertinent laws, in this case the Multiple-Use Sustained-Yield Act, the National Forest Management Act, and the Forest Service's Organic Act. Violations of the APA generally are characterized as acts that are "arbitrary and capricious."

The states—represented, incidentally, by California Deputy Attorney General Claudia Polsky, who had worked as an attorney at Earthjustice in the 1990s—argued that

> it was arbitrary and capricious for the Forest Service to reject a "preferred alternative" supported by three years of study and a detailed 700-page FEIS [final environmental impact statement] in favor of a policy wholly unanalyzed with regard to environmental consequences . . . and the Forest Service has not explained how it will achieve its institutional goal of reducing controversy and litigation surrounding roadless areas by rejecting a policy supported by 96% of the commenting public in favor of a policy opposed by 97% of that public.

Further, they pointed out that the Forest Service completely ignored the road-maintenance backlog problem in replacing a rule that discussed it extensively with one that discussed it not at all.

Six weeks after the states filed their complaint, Kristen Boyles, Tim Preso, and Tom Waldo filed a new suit on behalf of an even twenty conservation groups. That complaint mirrored the states' case and added the *failure-to-consult* accusation as a violation of the Endangered Species Act, stating that

when the Forest Service proposed to repeal the Roadless Rule, the agency
identified a number of concerns prompting it to take action. However,
the agency put before the public but a single proposal to address these
concerns: the wholesale repeal of the rule and its replacement with a
state petition process. There are other reasonable alternatives, retain-
ing the basic rule, that would address the agency's stated concerns at
least as well as the Roadless Repeal, with less adverse impact to the
environment....

The conservation groups then argued that the Forest Service violated the
Endangered Species Act by failing to consult with the USFWS and the NMFS
to determine whether the rule change might pose problems for protected
species. "When the Roadless Rule was originally promulgated," the groups
stated, "the Forest Service consulted with FWS and NMFS, but it failed to do
so when it repealed this protective rule. That failure violates the ESA."

Boyles, Preso, and Waldo then made an impassioned plea that the court
could, and should, restore Roadless Rule protections to the Tongass National
Forest, overriding the sweetheart deal the Bush administration had entered
into with the State of Alaska, which exempted the Tongass National Forest
from the Roadless Rule and froze the environmental intervenors out of the
settlement negotiations.

The case was assigned to Magistrate Judge Elizabeth Laporte in the Federal
District Court for Northern California, San Francisco. As mentioned in chapter 2, magistrates are hired by district courts to ease workloads; they do not
serve for life, and are not confirmed by the Senate. In general, decisions by
magistrates are reviewed by a district court judge, but in this case all sides
agreed that any appeal of a ruling by Judge Laporte would go straight to the
Ninth Circuit Court of Appeals.

Judge Laporte, a graduate of Yale Law School, was appointed a magistrate
by the district court in 1998, having served as an administrative law judge in
the California Department of Insurance. She would prove to be a quick study,
swiftly learning the gnarled and tangled history of the case she had been
assigned, not to mention the cases languishing in various states of limbo
across the country.

The Petition Polka I 15

By December 2005, the Bush administration's approach to the Roadless Area Conservation Rule, the state petition process, was beginning to move forward. The Roadless Area Conservation National Advisory Committee (RACNAC) met, and Dale Harris of the Montana Wilderness Association and Greg Schaefer of Arch Coal were named cochairmen. Apart from that agreement, there were wrangles over how to proceed, whether to try to work by consensus, and myriad other administrative details.

The first petition submitted to the committee came from North Carolina, soon followed by petitions from Virginia and South Carolina. Clearly it was time to have another meeting. The following is an account I prepared following the next two-day meeting.

Report on the Roadless Area Conservation National Advisory Committee (RACNAC) Meeting: May 8–9, 2006, Washington, DC

The committee consists of thirteen people from quite a diversity of interests. Under Secretary Mark Rey selected them from forty applicants, some nominated by themselves, some nominated by others. They all represented special interests or filled a specialized role in the proceedings:

- Beef—Jeff Eisenberg of the National Cattlemen's Beef Association
- Ski—Geraldine Link of the National Ski Areas Association
- Timber—Jim Riley of the Intermountain Forest Association
- Coal—Greg Schaefer of the National Coal Association and Arch Coal
- Snowmobile—Adena Cook of the Blue Ribbon Coalition
- Wilderness West—Dale Harris of the Montana Wilderness Association
- Wilderness East—Ray Vaughan of Wildlaw in Alabama
- The Expert—Chris Wood of Trout Unlimited and an advisor to Mike Dombeck during preparation and review of the 2001 rule
- The Biologist—Todd Schulke of the Center for Biological Diversity
- Trout—Paul Hansen of the Izaak Walton League (who didn't attend the second day)
- State—Darin Bird, deputy director of the Utah Department of Natural Resources

Two others who were chosen for the committee, Robert Cope and Denny Scott, representing county commissioners and labor, respectively, didn't attend the meetings.

For the second meeting they reviewed petitions that had been received from Virginia, North Carolina, and South Carolina, all of which asked for complete protection of their roadless areas. By western standards, these national forestlands are small (VA: 374,000 acres; NC: 174,000 acres; SC: 7,500 acres). These petitions asked that the provisions of the 2001 Roadless Rule be reinstated for their forests. So on the first day, members took turns presenting the petitions to the committee. Mark Rey was there, sitting quietly at the side of the room, listening attentively, not saying much. (As an aside, letters sent by Oregon Governor Ted Kulongoski and Washington Governor Christine Gregoire asking for reimposition of the 2001 rule for their states came up, and Rey said that he had refused their request. Reason: The 2001 rule doesn't exist anymore, and the litigation muddied the situation.)

After representatives from the three petitioning states made their pitches, the committee wrangled for a few hours about how to proceed. Should they suggest a remand (Ski, Beef, and Wilderness East are lawyers and, along with Timber and the Expert, will dominate the deliberations) if they have problems? Ask governors to provide more information? Mark Rey had told them at the organizing meeting that they could do absolutely whatever they wanted.

The following points of contention came up again and again:

References to the 2001 Roadless Rule. Ski demanded, insisted, ordered that all references to the 2001 rule be expunged since it is not in force and is five years old. Others pointed out politely that the 2001 rule represents a vast amount of work and information and is what the 2005 rule is based on, having no environmental documentation of its own. They eventually agreed that they would suggest to Mark Rey that he ask the states to use the actual language of the parts of the 2001 rule that pertain to their situations, as they move forward with memorandums of understanding (MOUs), scoping, and new National Environmental Protection Act (NEPA) processes.

Public involvement. The Bush administration's 2005 rule does not actually require public involvement but simply asks for a report on any steps the states have taken to assess public attitudes about the rule, as the Expert reminded the committee many times. The preamble, however, as Ski pointed out several times, assumes that the states will take the public's temperature. The three states whose petitions were being considered this week all made reference to the comments they logged about the original Roadless Rule, but Ski and others said those comments didn't count. Snowmobile said repeatedly that NEPA is not a popularity contest; she is clearly sick of hearing about the millions of comments that supported the 2001 rule and opposed the 2005 rule.

Whether all interest groups had been consulted. Here it became clear that the proroadless side was far better organized in all three states than the commercial interests. Timber, Beef, Ski, and Snowmobile all argued that the states should have made a greater effort to reach out to their industries (or, in the case of Snowmobile, to the motorized-recreation crowd). This is a theme that will return.

Moratorium. The petitions, plus letters to Mark Rey that the governors of Oregon and Washington sent last fall, ask for a moratorium on activities in roadless areas until the petition process runs its course. Again, the commodity faction of the RACNAC opposes this. Wilderness East says that Mark Rey has sent a new directive to his forest supervisors urging them to assure the governors of their states that they won't approve any new projects in inventoried roadless areas (IRAS) without consulting the states first. Mat Jacobson of Heritage Forests said later that there are twenty projects underway in IRAS now, some of which are mistakes. This may come up again.

Compatibility with forest plans. In these three states, existing management plans seem to protect most IRAS from road building and logging. In all cases, the states are working closely with the Forest Service and seem confident that they can arrive at acceptable compromises when there are differences. The Expert and others on the proroadless side of the fence pointed out that states can ask for whatever they want; the other faction continued to urge states and the Forest Service to reach common ground. But if they reach common ground, why bother with petitions?

Nationalism. This is a bit abstract but may be important. RACNAC is held up as proof that the petition process is a national exercise (in response to the "taking the national out of national forests" line)—the committee is charged with bringing a national perspective to the proceedings. Yet Snowmobile and others said repeatedly that each petition should be taken on its own, that the petitions shouldn't be compared with one another, and that the committee's job was to help the states achieve what they want.

Economic impact on communities and individuals. This is Beef's biggest concern, and he will urge that this be explored and considered in all cases.

Loss of forest and agricultural land to sprawl and development. The Expert kept asking for data to demonstrate the growing value of preserving what undeveloped lands remain.

Growing demand for developed recreation. Ski responded that the demand for ski areas and such is growing as well and should be measured.

Noninventoried areas. Wilderness East said that the governor of Alabama will petition to have one five-thousand acre area added to the list of protected roadless areas. It was left out of the inventory and should have been included. This could cause a ruckus.

At the end of the meeting, all three petitions were given a provisional thumbs-up. Letters will go to Mark Rey and Agriculture Secretary Mike Johanns with suggestions on parts that should be strengthened as the process moves toward MOUS. Beef and the Biologist will draft the Virginia letter, Timber and Wilderness East will write the letter for North Carolina, and Snowmobile and the Expert will write South Carolina. The deadline for getting recommendations to Mark Rey for Virginia is the end of May; for North Carolina, sometime in June; and for South Carolina, sometime in July. The Forest Service will then have ninety days to give a formal response to the states.

Colorado and Idaho have been given money to help with their comment-gathering activities. New Mexico has written three letters asking for money and hasn't had an answer, probably because of the lawsuit and because New Mexico Governor Bill Richardson is a Democrat. Several states are debating whether to petition; others are getting their petitions ready. RACNAC members seem to expect another dozen or so petitions to be submitted. The committee agreed to try to set meetings every two months or so, assuming they can find dates that work for everyone. The meetings may be held elsewhere, especially when the big western states join the party.

As it turned out, only seven states submitted petitions: North Carolina, South Carolina, Virginia, California, New Mexico, Idaho, and Colorado. The first five requested total protection for all roadless areas in those states. The Idaho and Colorado petitions called for some protection and some exploitation. The whole applecart was about to be overturned, however, out in California.

The Bush Rule
Is Blocked

16

On September 20, 2006, Judge Laporte ruled that the Forest Service had violated the National Environmental Policy Act (NEPA) by failing to prepare an environmental study when it issued its new Roadless Area Conservation Rule. Specifically, she said that

> the question for the Court is not, of course, which rule is preferable; that is for the Executive Branch. Nor is there any doubt that the Forest Service has the authority to change policies from a uniform national approach strongly protecting roadless areas from human encroachment to a more localized approach permitting more roads and logging, provided that it follows the proper procedures. Rather, the question is whether the Forest Service complied with the procedures mandated by Congress for consideration of potential environmental impacts prior to changing course, or was exempt from doing so. The resolution of this question turns on whether the State Petitions Rule is merely procedural, or instead constitutes a substantive repeal of the Roadless Rule in favor of a different scheme for managing roadless areas that raises substantial questions whether the change will significantly impact the environment or may affect endangered or threatened species. For the reason set forth below, including significant guidance that the court of appeals

provided in Kootenai Tribe, *this Court concludes that the Forest Service failed adequately to consider the environmental and species impacts when it issued the State Petitions Rule, in violation of* NEPA *and* ESA *[Endangered Species Act].*

The *Kootenai Tribe* case was, of course, the case from Idaho, where the district court judge, Edward Lodge, found the 2001 Roadless Rule illegal under NEPA and enjoined it nationwide. Judge Lodge's injunction was overturned by the Ninth Circuit Court of Appeals, which signaled quite clearly that it thought the rule was pretty solid. Judge Laporte wrote that "while the Court of Appeals reviewed the validity of the Roadless Rule in the context of a preliminary injunction, it explained in considerable detail its conclusion on that record that the Forest Service had provided adequate notice and opportunity to comment and properly considered a reasonable range of alternatives under NEPA."

Judge Laporte also made reference to Judge Brimmer in Wyoming, who would be so scornful about the ruling she was in the process of explaining, that "in July 2003, the Wyoming district court issued a nationwide permanent injunction against the Roadless Rule.... The Wyoming court acknowledged the Ninth Circuit's decision in *Kootenai Tribe*, but declined to follow that precedent." She quoted Judge Brimmer, who had written that "this Court finds the *Kootenai Tribe* opinion to be of limited persuasive value. Moreover, because this Court is unable to discern what NEPA opinions *Kootenai Tribe* overruled, this Court will refrain from relying on any Ninth Circuit NEPA opinions as persuasive authority." Judge Brimmer's antipathy toward the Ninth Circuit is well known, on a par with his opinion of the Clinton administration.

On the Endangered Species Act claim, Judge Laporte wrote that

the Forest Service violated the ESA *by failing to engage in the consultation process before issuing the State Petitions Rule. Again, in reaching this conclusion, the Court does not hold that regardless of the substance or scope of a Forest Service regulation, its repeal automatically triggers consultation obligations under* ESA. *Nor does the Court hold that engaging in* ESA *consultation in promulgating the original rule always necessitates consultation of the repeal of that rule. Rather, here, under the circumstances of this case,* ESA *consultation with regard to the State Petitions Rule was required.*

The one facet of Judge Laporte's ruling that disappointed the states and the environmental organizations was her refusal to reinstate the 2001 rule on the Tongass National Forest in Alaska. This was a complicated procedural question—whether the Tongass Amendment, the deal cut between the Forest Service and the State of Alaska—should be honored. Judge Laporte ruled that it should be:

> *After carefully considering all of the parties' and amici's arguments and balancing the equities, the Court has determined that . . . the proper course . . . is to reinstate the prior Roadless Rule with the 2003 Tongass Amendment. . . . Under different circumstances than presented here, such as when a prior regulation had never taken effect, or was only intended to be temporary or when the rule held invalid had been an integral part of a regulatory scheme, departure from the general rule . . . would be warranted. . . . None of these special circumstances apply in this case. The Roadless Rule was not temporary, it did take effect, and the proponents of the State Petitions Rule do not contend that it is an integral part of an overall regulatory scheme. To the contrary, Defendants urge reinstatement of the forest plans as a remedy. . . . Because the Tongass Amendment was part of the rule that was previously in force before the State Petitions Rule, reinstatement of the Amendment follows the Ninth Circuit's guidance. . . .*

In other words, the fact that the Tongass amendment—the agreement between the Forest Service and the State of Alaska to exclude the Tongass National Forest from the Roadless Rule—had been in place at the time the Bush petition rule was announced, meant that the exclusion of the Tongass would remain in force.

The clever maneuvering between the State of Alaska and the Bush administration had managed to remove the Tongass from the rule's reach. Environmental groups vowed to fight every last timber sale that might be proposed in the Tongass' roadless areas.

Otherwise, the states and the conservation groups were ecstatic. The 2001 Roadless Rule was once again in force.

Or was it?

The administration, unwilling to concede defeat, produced an analysis of the ruling which said that since the rule had been enjoined by Judge Lodge in 2001 and Judge Brimmer in 2003, that only road building suggested after September 20, 2006, when Judge Laporte issued her ruling, would be prohibited. In particular, this was about some 327 oil and gas leases, mainly in the Rocky Mountains, that had been approved in roadless areas between 2001 and 2006 and on which work had not yet begun. The environmental groups filed a motion with the court calling the administration's argument nonsense.

Lawyers for both sides returned to Judge Laporte's courtroom for clarification, which she produced on November 29. She dismissed the government's argument out of hand, reaffirming that the 2001 rule, exempting the Tongass, was the law of the land and that only projects approved before January 2001 in roadless areas could proceed:

> Defendants [the federal government] provide no authority for applying the Roadless Rule only as of the date of the Court's Opinion. Contrary to Defendants' argument, the fact that the Roadless Rule when adopted in January 2001 applied to permits and projects undertaken after that date, as rules typically do, in no way supports delaying its reinstatement until the unrelated date in 2006 of this Court's ruling that Defendants unlawfully repealed the Rule, rather than the date of the unlawful repeal. The Court specifically reinstated the Roadless Rule as it stood with the Tongass Amendment, as of the date of its unlawful repeal by the State Petitions Rule.

The government continued to argue until February 6, 2007, when Judge Laporte issued a final and explicit injunction repealing the 2005 Bush rule and reinstating the 2001 Clinton rule, minus the Tongass. The only recourse left to the Forest Service was now to lodge an appeal with the Ninth Circuit. It did so on the very day the statute of limitations for an appeal would have run out. The court ordered the government to file its opening brief at the end of July 2007.

The brief didn't appear until September 14. The arguments were interesting. According to the government's analysis of the timeline, the Clinton rule was in force for only three months—between when the Ninth Circuit lifted Judge Lodge's injunction and when Judge Brimmer enjoined the rule nationwide. This meant that the rule "was never meaningfully in force prior to the adoption of the State Petitions Rule," according to this line of argument, that "the Roadless Rule was not part of the regulatory status quo." Further, the Forest Service argued, "The Rule does not establish policy for roadless areas or dictate the use of any particular roadless area." And therefore the petition rule "would have no effects on listed species or critical habitat and was not subject to consultation under the ESA.... the district court abused its discretion in 'reinstating' the Roadless Rule."

The government was arguing, in essence, that in replacing the Clinton rule with the petitions rule it was not "repealing" the original rule because it was under injunction, and therefore it didn't exist, or had existed for only a few months (seven months, rather than three, at any rate). The key here is *repeal*. If what the Bush administration did was repeal the Clinton rule, the National Environmental Policy Act clearly required environmental studies, and the Administrative Procedure Act would come into play as well. The government argued instead that it wasn't repealing the rule because the rule was gone. In their opposition briefs, the states and the environmental groups all but scoffed:

> *Underlying the agency's argument is the notion that if it does not call its action a repeal, it will cease to be a repeal ("USDA's intent to withdraw the enjoined Roadless Rule does not mean that USDA 'repealed' the Roadless Rule's substantive protections.") Indeed, throughout its opening brief the word "repeal" is placed in quotes. Neither synonym gymnastics nor excessive punctuation can change the fact that . . . the Forest Service substantively repealed the Roadless Rule when the Forest Service promulgated the State Petitions Rule.*
>
> *Having successfully argued that the replacement of the Roadless Rule rendered moot the Wyoming litigation, the Forest Service here argues exactly the opposite: that the Wyoming judgment obviated any need to repeal the rule. The agency cannot sustain these contradictory positions in different courts.*
>
> *The issue before this Court under NEPA is whether it was reasonable for the Forest Service to conclude that the Roadless Repeal was merely procedural and therefore categorically exempt from NEPA. For the ESA, the question is whether the Forest Service was justified in its determination that the repeal would have "no effect" on endangered species. A critical link in the agency's argument under both statutes is that the Wyoming injunction dissolved the rule, so that the "state petitions"*

rule was merely procedural and in fact did not even repeal the Roadless Rule.... The repeal of the Roadless Rule and the mooting of all pending litigation about it had an enormous potential impact on millions of acres of national forest land.

The "meaningfully in force" standard, the environmental groups went on, is a fabrication, an invention that has no basis in law.

In plain English, what the environmental groups (and the states, in a separate brief) argued was that in one forum, the Forest Service argued that it was the court (Judge Brimmer) that nullified the Roadless Rule so there was nothing to repeal (this being the argument presented to the Ninth Circuit), while also arguing (in the Tenth Circuit) that the agency itself had replaced the existing Roadless Rule and, therefore, the appeal of Judge Brimmer's order should be dismissed. The four states asked the court to block ("collaterally estop") the Forest Service from talking out of both sides of its mouth.

A timber company and a four-wheel-drive club that intervened to help the Forest Service submitted their own briefs, arguing that the state petitions rule itself has no environmental impact, the Roadless Rule was never meaningfully in effect, and other assertions closely in line with the government's position.

The Ninth Circuit, with a packed docket, accepted the briefs. Oral argument was set for October 20, 2008.

Meanwhile, Wyoming sought to salvage its position elsewhere, to undo Judge Laporte's reinstatement of the 2001 Clinton Roadless Rule. The previous autumn, immediately following Judge Laporte's decision, lawyers for the state, led by then attorney general Pat Crank, filed a motion in Judge Brimmer's court asking him, in essence, to reimpose his 2003 injunction, effectively overruling Judge Laporte, a highly irregular maneuver that could violate the ideal of comity for which federal courts generally strive.

It wasn't quite that simple, of course. What they asked was that Judge Brimmer take it upon himself to lift the vacatur order from the Tenth Circuit, issued in July 2005, that had wiped his 2003 injunction against the 2001 rule off the books. The lawyers cited an obscure federal rule that allows this action in extremely rare cases. Lawyers for the conservation groups—in California, Oregon, New Mexico, and Washington—were quietly watching from the sidelines at this point—told Judge Brimmer that he had no authority to grant such a motion, and that if Wyoming wanted the vacatur lifted it would have to ask the Tenth Circuit to do so.

Judge Brimmer's bailiff called his courtroom to order at 10 a.m. on Friday, May 25, 2007. The judge climbed to the bench. Wyoming Attorney General Pat Crank was there to argue the case himself for the State. Opposing him were Clay Samford, from the Department of Justice, and Jim Angell of Earthjustice, representing the conservation organizations. The Bush administration hadn't suddenly become a fan of the original Roadless Rule, but simply felt that Judge Brimmer didn't have the authority to defy this order from the appeals court.

Judge Brimmer immediately surprised everyone by scolding the Bush administration for not writing an environmental impact statement to go along with its petition rule, put into place in May 2005. He also made quite clear his skepticism over whether he in fact could ignore the vacatur order and reinstate the injunction.

If the federal government's lawyer showed no enthusiasm for the old rule, the judge showed utter contempt. He referred to it repeatedly as "Dr. Frankenstein's monster," and implied that Judge Laporte had somehow been "chosen for that role," enjoining the Bush rule and reinstating the Clinton rule, as if nefarious Clintonians and elitist greens held sway over federal judges in the Northern District of California.

Nonetheless, Judge Brimmer gave Pat Crank a difficult time, asked hardly any questions of the federal government or the conservation groups, and said he'd rule in a week or ten days.

Meanwhile, a solid group of more than 150 congressmen and senators (led in the Senate by Republican John Warner of Virginia and Democrat Maria Cantwell of Washington; in the House by Democrat Jay Inslee of Washington) introduced a bill that would make the 2001 rule the law of the land. They did not expect the bill to pass quickly, but saw it as a way to rally further public support. Organizers with the Heritage Forests Campaign and dozens of other groups urged their members to press their legislators to become cosponsors of the bill.

Judge Brimmer made good on his promise late on June 7, 2007, reluctantly issuing an order denying Wyoming's motion. The judge repeated what he had said in open court about the Bush administration's possible violation of federal law in issuing its own Roadless Rule with no environmental analysis, and then said, *this Court is extremely perplexed over how the California court could resurrect the Clinton Roadless Rule. The Clinton Roadless Rule did not comply with NEPA and this Court held it invalid. This Court is troubled and questions the authority of the California court to raise this rule back to life and force. Clearly, a California Magistrate Judge could have no right, by way of appeal, to reverse this Court's decision, which still stands, even though the Tenth Circuit ordered the case dismissed. . . . Judge Laporte plainly did not have the authority to do so or the power to revive a once dead rule.*

But no one had asked the judge to rule on whether Judge Laporte had the power to resurrect the rule. The question before Judge Brimmer was an extremely narrow legal question—whether he could overturn a directive from the appeals court above him—and he reluctantly concluded that he could not. He wrote that "Wyoming's proper procedural remedy is now to inform the Tenth Circuit of the California ruling and ask that the circuit court recall its mandate." In other words, Wyoming should go back to the appeals court in Denver and ask that court to revive the challenge to the Clinton rule in Judge Brimmer's court.

Accordingly, Wyoming returned to the Tenth Circuit and asked that court to reopen the case given the dramatically changed circumstances. The environmental groups did not oppose that motion—being eager to get the matters resolved and hopeful that the appeals court would overrule Judge Brimmer and come down approximately as the Ninth Circuit judges had. The Tenth Circuit, however, declined to reopen the case. A new case was filed by Wyoming in Judge Brimmer's court and immediately joined by the environmental groups. Wyoming's suit was nearly identical to its original suit, even using parts of the original brief. It asked Judge Brimmer to issue, or reissue, an injunction to block the 2001 Roadless Rule throughout the country, citing Judge Laporte's injunction as the reason.

The Petition Polka II 17

JUDGE LAPORTE'S INJUNCTION had thrown the petition process into chaos; in fact, it had thrown the petition process and the Roadless Area Conservation National Advisory Committee—RACNAC—into legal limbo, at best.

The Forest Service quickly invited the states to refile their petitions under the Administrative Procedure Act (APA) and took steps to reconvene the committee. RACNAC was duly reconstituted, with all members staying on board.

All five states that had filed petitions under the Bush rule declined the APA suggestion. The five—North Carolina, South Carolina, Virginia, New Mexico, and California—had asked for complete protection for their roadless areas and were therefore happy that Judge Laporte's injunction appeared to have restored protection for their forests, though in the case of California, the Sierra Club's Mary Wells said in an email that state groups and Governor Schwarzenegger felt that California's petition would have afforded stronger protection than the 2001 Roadless Rule, had the petition been approved.

Still, given the repeal of the Bush rule, there was no reason to file a new petition, which would only open a new rule-making process that could only water down the protection their forests had just regained.

The two states that did choose to press forward with APA petitions were Idaho and Colorado. Both those states had canvassed public opinion within their borders and found a wide variety of views. They decided to carry on with new petitions.

Oregon and Washington had submitted petitions that sought to expedite action on their earlier requests for complete protection for their national forests. Mark Rey summarily denied both.

Idaho has the largest block of inventoried roadless areas (IRAS) outside Alaska, more than nine million acres. The job of canvassing public opinion fell to the lieutenant governor, Jim Risch, who would shortly become governor of Idaho upon the appointment of Governor Dirk Kempthorne to be secretary of the interior, replacing Gale Norton. Risch would decline to run for a full term as governor himself, but return as lieutenant governor when Butch Otter was elected governor in 2006.

The Idaho petition had been submitted two days before Judge Laporte's injunction was handed down. It called for opening up more than 80 percent of national forest land in the state to one or another sort of development, according to an analysis by the Heritage Forests Campaign. Idaho has a vigorous environmental community, led by the Idaho Conservation League, but it is an overwhelmingly Republican state these days, though its past featured a staunch Democratic environmentalist senator named Frank Church, and a governor, Cecil Andrus, who would serve as secretary of the interior under Jimmy Carter.

On October 5, 2006, Governor Risch submitted Idaho's petition to RACNAC under the authority of the APA, the same petition the state had submitted under the Bush Roadless Rule. Angry letters poured into the statehouse in Boise from conservation groups, highly critical of the petition, and they seemed to have had their desired effect. On November 30, Governor Risch appeared personally at a RACNAC meeting to present the state's petition. He explained that he was asking that three million of Idaho's more than nine million roadless acres be given even stronger protection than the Clinton Roadless Rule provided, that five and a half million acres receive the same level of protection, and that only a half million acres be given less protection than that provided by the 2001 rule. By several accounts it was a shock to the members of RACNAC. The committee discussed the petition and forwarded it to Mark Rey with a recommendation that it move forward, reflecting the comments made by Governor Risch.

The Bush administration, however, soon issued a draft environmental impact statement (DEIS) and draft rule that did not reflect the governor's statement, instead loosening restrictions on logging, mining, and other development on about six million acres. The drafts were open for public comment; by late spring, 140,000 comments had been submitted, 100,000 of them objecting to the proposed changes in the draft DEIS and draft rule.

In Colorado, Governor Bill Owens, a Republican, had been an outspoken opponent of the 2001 Roadless Rule. He appointed a task force to recommend provisions of a petition to submit under the Bush Roadless Rule. The task force developed a petition that was a compromise between what the governor would have preferred and what the environmental community wanted, with enhanced access to some roadless areas for ski resorts, grazing-related activities, and other kinds of development. The petition was submitted just before Judge Laporte overturned the Bush rule then resubmitted under the APA.

The following November, Bill Ritter, a Democrat, was elected governor of Colorado. As is customary in such situations, the Forest Service asked if the new governor would like to withdraw or revise the petition, which he did. The substitute petition offered slightly more protection for Colorado's roadless areas. Governor Ritter called it an insurance policy to be in place should the Clinton rule eventually lose in the courts.

The Colorado petition was considered by the advisory committee, and on August 8, 2007, it made twenty recommendations for strengthening it. In December 2007, the Forest Service produced an advance notice of proposed rule making, seeking public comments on the proposed rule, which included none of RACNAC's twenty suggestions. Eighty thousand people submitted comments in opposition to the draft. Final rules are expected to be issued before the end of the Bush presidency in January 2009.

The Game Is Up 18

THIS BOOK is going to press just days after the election of Barack Obama, who supported reinstatement of the 2001 Roadless Rule during the campaign. Time will tell. Appeals and other challenges are still pending in court, and two petitions (Idaho's and Colorado's) are nearing final approval and may well be challenged in court, so it will be some time before all the i's are dotted and the t's are crossed in the roadless saga. If the next presidential administration is sympathetic to the idea of keeping roadless areas roadless, and Congress feels the same way, then it is possible, if not certain, that the 2001 rule, conceived of by Steve Kallick, Niel Lawrence, Marty Hayden, Mike Francis, Jim Jontz, and others; hatched by Mike Dombeck, Jim Lyons, Katie McGinty, George Frampton, John Podesta, and Bill Clinton; supported by millions of Americans with the organizing assistance of much of the environmental movement; fueled by the considerable resources of the Pew Charitable Trusts; and defended by a brilliant team of lawyers will become the law of the land. Still, continuing legal challenges may be anticipated from states like Wyoming and Idaho and commercial timber companies, and possibly some tribes, though with a Justice Department vigorously defending the rule it stands a pretty good chance of surviving. If, however, as Mark Rey suggests, it should end up before the Supreme Court, anything could happen.

Regardless of all that, informed consensus seems to be that the forest defenders have carried the day, that drastic overcutting of the national forests is a thing of the past, and that most roadless areas will remain inviolate. Skirmishes will continue no doubt, but the will of the public is certainly clear. With local exceptions based on concerns about jobs, or pride, or simple bullheadedness, the public is overwhelmingly in favor of protecting national forest roadless areas and knows how to make its feelings known. Things can always change, but for now, at any rate, the roadless forests seem to be able to go back to being forests—home to a wide variety of plants and animals, to hunters and hikers and anglers, producers of vital water for humans and wildlife alike—and take a rest from being considered candidates for tree farms.

It's fair to say that the activity surrounding the Roadless Area Conservation Rule is a high-water mark in environmental activism, having engaged more people than anything before it, enlisting the power of philanthropy and the legal system in the service of the greater public good on behalf of the environment we all depend on. A big question is whether it can be replicated on other issues. Pew's Steve Kallick sounds a pessimistic note and thinks the environmental movement—that amorphous, unwieldy, imperfect, and hard-to-define creature—has failed to understand and take advantage of the implications of the Roadless Rule experience, which is that, with smart planning and extraordinary effort—plus financial support from Pew and other sources—great things can be accomplished.

In retrospect, it's also fair to say that Mark Rey and company miscalculated in the evident strategy of letting the courts "take down" the 2001 Roadless Rule and in failing to do any environmental analysis of the substitute rule put forward in 2005. They could easily have torpedoed the Roadless Rule if they'd been a little more careful, as Judge Laporte acknowledged in her opinion, and others admit in conversation. That was a bit of good fortune for the forests that might not be repeated should the pendulum swing back again; both sides have learned many lessons from this battle.

Appendix 1

Inventoried Roadless Areas: By State, in Thousands of Acres

Alabama	13
Alaska	14,779
Arizona	1,174
Arkansas	95
California	4,416
Colorado	4,433
Connecticut	0
Delaware	0
Florida	50
Georgia	63
Hawaii	0
Idaho	9,322
Illinois	11
Indiana	8
Iowa	0
Kansas	0
Kentucky	3
Louisiana	7
Maine	6
Maryland	0
Massachusetts	0
Michigan	16

Minnesota	62
Mississippi	3
Missouri	25
Montana	6,397
Nebraska	0
Nevada	3,186
New Hampshire	235
New Jersey	0
New Mexico	1,597
New York	0
North Carolina	172
North Dakota	266
Ohio	0
Oklahoma	13
Oregon	1,965
Pennsylvania	25
Rhode Island	0
South Carolina	8
South Dakota	80
Tennessee	85
Texas	4
Utah	4,013
Vermont	25
Virginia	394
Washington	2,015
West Virginia	202
Wisconsin	69
Wyoming	3,257
Total	**58,518**

Note: Puerto Rico has a national forest with 24,000 acres of roadless areas. This figure is included in the total above.

Source: Figures compiled by, and are available from, the USDA *Forest Service.*
http://roadless.fs.fed.us/documents/feis/data/sheets/acres/appendix_state_acres.html

Appendix 2

Timeline of Milestones in the Campaign to Protect National Forest Roadless Areas

1891	The Creative Act: Congress authorizes the president to establish forest reserves on federal public domain lands.
1897	The Organic Act: Congress gives the secretary of the interior broad power to regulate and protect the forest reserves.
1905	The Transfer Act: Congress transfers the forest reserves to the U.S. Department of Agriculture.
1907	President Theodore Roosevelt triples the amount of national forestland, from 46 million acres to 132 million acres.
1924	Forest Service establishes the Gila Primitive Area in New Mexico at the behest of Aldo Leopold.
1926	Forest Service Chief William Greeley directs the agency to inventory all national forest roadless areas. The inventory identifies 55 million acres of roadless areas ranging in size from 230,000 acres to 7 million acres.
1927	National forest road system reaches 35,000 miles, up from 5,000 miles in 1907.
1929	Forest Service formalizes the Primitive Areas category.

1933	Forest Service establishes sixty-three primitive areas totaling 8.4 million acres.
1939	Forest Service establishes Wilderness Area and Wild Area categories, where roads, logging, and motorized vehicles are prohibited.
1956	First wilderness bill is introduced by Senator Hubert Humphrey of Minnesota.
1964	The Wilderness Act is signed into law. It establishes the National Wilderness Preservation System and includes 9.1 million acres in the system. It also directs the Forest Service to conduct an inventory of its lands and recommend additions to the system.
1972	Forest Service releases its Roadless Area Review and Evaluation (RARE), which identifies 56 million acres of roadless land and proposes 12.3 million acres for consideration by Congress for addition to roadless areas.
1977	Forest Service undertakes a second inventory, known as RARE II.
1979	RARE II is released. It identifies 62 million roadless acres, nearly one-third of the national forest system. The Forest Service recommends 15 million acres be added to the wilderness system.
1982	Ninth Circuit invalidates much of RARE II as a violation of the National Environmental Policy Act.
1988	Forest Service road system reaches 355,000 miles.
July 1997	Congress comes within one vote of eliminating the Forest Service's road budget.
November 1997	President Clinton announces that the Forest Service is developing a science-based policy for managing roadless areas.
December 1997	One hundred and sixty-nine scientists write to President Clinton in support of roadless area protection.
January 1998	Forest Service Chief Mike Dombeck proposes an eighteen-month moratorium on new road building in most roadless areas. The proposal excludes forests with updated management plans, including the Tongass National Forest in Alaska and nineteen forests in the Pacific Northwest.

March 1, 1999	Forest Service adopts an eighteen-month moratorium on new roads as outlined in Dombeck's January 1998 proposal.
June 1999	Three hundred religious leaders write to President Clinton urging a strong and effective policy to protect roadless areas.
June 1999	More than a quarter-million comments in the form of postcards, letters, and email messages are delivered to the administration expressing support for a strong national forest roadless-area protection policy.
October 1999	Forest Service publishes a notice of intent to prepare an environmental impact statement on roadless-area management in the *Federal Register* and initiates a sixty-day comment period on what the scope of the policy ought to be.
October 13, 1999	President Clinton directs the Forest Service to initiate a rulemaking process to determine how best to manage roadless areas.
December 1999	Public comment period closes with 400,000 comments received.
May 9, 2000	Forest Service releases a draft environmental impact statement. The preferred alternative would ban roads, but not logging, and excludes the Tongass National Forest.
May–June 2000	Forest Service conducts hearings and accepts public comments, which, counting the scoping comments, number 1.6 million, by orders of magnitude the most comments ever received for a federal rule making.
January 5, 2001	President Clinton and Agriculture Secretary Dan Glickman announce the Roadless Area Conservation Rule prohibiting road building and logging on all inventoried roadless areas, including the Tongass National Forest. Exceptions are made for fire suppression and other management activities and for some previously approved timber sales.
January 5, 2001	Boise Cascade and others file suit in federal court in Idaho to challenge the Roadless Rule.
January 9, 2001	State of Idaho files suit in federal court in Idaho challenging the rule.
January 12, 2001	The Roadless Area Conservation Rule is published in the *Federal Register*.

January 20, 2001	George W. Bush is inaugurated president. Andrew Card, the new White House chief of staff, circulates a memo directing cabinet secretaries to freeze any rules or regulations that haven't yet gone into effect.
January 31, 2001	Alaska files suit challenging the rule.
February 5, 2001	Agriculture Secretary Ann Veneman postpones the effective date of the Roadless Rule to May 12, 2001, citing the directive from Andrew Card.
March 28, 2001	Colorado files a friend-of-the-court brief in support of Idaho's lawsuit.
March 30, 2001	Bush administration does not defend the Roadless Rule and asks the court to wait for the administration to complete its review and file a status report by May 4, 2001.
April 20, 2001	Utah files a lawsuit to challenge the Roadless Rule.
April 20, 2001	Timber industry coalition, led by the American Forest and Paper Association, files suit in the District of Columbia to challenge the Roadless Rule.
May 3, 2001	Montana and Wyoming files friend-of-the-court briefs in support of Idaho's lawsuit.
May 4, 2001	Bush administration announces its intention to implement the Roadless Rule with "responsible amendments" by the end of June.
May 8, 2001	Four counties in North Dakota file a lawsuit challenging the Roadless Rule.
May 10, 2001	Judge Edward Lodge issues a preliminary nationwide injunction blocking implementation of the rule.
May 19, 2001	Wyoming files suit to challenge the Roadless Rule.
May 21, 2001	Ninth Circuit agrees to hear the appeal on an expedited basis.
May 31, 2001	Environmental groups appeal Judge Lodge's injunction to the Ninth Circuit Court of Appeals. The Forest Service does not appeal.
June 6, 2001	Montana attorney general files a friend-of-the-court brief with the Ninth Circuit in support of the environmental organizations.

June 7, 2001	Forest Service Chief Dale Bosworth reserves for himself the final decision on logging proposals in roadless areas.
July 10, 2001	Bush administration issues an advance notice of proposed rule making, seeking comments on how the Roadless Rule might be altered.
September 10, 2001	North Dakota files suit challenging the Roadless Rule.
October 1, 2001	Judge Jackson grants federal government's motion to stay indefinitely the two Roadless Rule lawsuits filed in Washington, DC.
October 15, 2001	The Ninth Circuit Court of Appeals hears oral argument in the appeal of Judge Lodge's injunction.
December 12, 2002	The Ninth Circuit reverses Judge Lodge and lifts his injunction against the Roadless Rule.
March 26, 2003	The Forest Roads Working Group recommends that the Forest Service implement the Roadless Rule and discontinue efforts to amend it.
June 12, 2003	Bush administration announces that it will propose changes to the Roadless Rule to exempt the Tongass and Chugach national forests in Alaska.
July 14, 2003	Wyoming District Court Judge Clarence Brimmer rules that the Roadless Rule is illegal and issues a nationwide injunction blocking it from taking effect. Environmental intervenor groups file an appeal with the Tenth Circuit Court of Appeals.
September 12, 2003	Justice Department announces that it will not appeal Judge Brimmer's injunction.
November 12, 2003	Justice Department files a friend-of-the-court brief with the Tenth Circuit urging that court to deny the intervenors' appeal.
December 23, 2003	Forest Service exempts the Tongass National Forest from the Roadless Rule.
July 12, 2004	Secretary of Agriculture Ann Veneman announces that the administration will propose replacing the Roadless Rule with a state petition process.
July 16, 2004	Draft petition rule is published in the *Federal Register*.

May 4, 2005	The Tenth Circuit Court of Appeals hears oral argument in the appeal of Judge Brimmer's injunction.
May 5, 2005	Bush administration announces that it is replacing the 2001 Roadless Rule with a new state petition rule.
May 13, 2005	Bush administration issues its final regulation repealing the Roadless Rule and replacing it with a state petition process.
July 11, 2005	The Tenth Circuit Court of Appeals dismisses the appeal of the Wyoming district court decision and vacates the decision on the ground that the case has been made moot by the repeal of the Roadless Rule.
August 28, 2005	California, Oregon, and New Mexico file suit challenging the state petition rule and the repeal of the original rule.
October 5, 2005	Twenty environmental groups file suit making many of the same allegations as the states' suit filed August 28.
December 14, 2005	Roadless Area Conservation National Advisory Committee holds its first meeting.
December 22, 2005	Virginia files a petition with the Forest Service seeking protection for all roadless areas in its national forests.
February 9, 2006	Washington joins the lawsuit filed by California, Oregon, and New Mexico as a plaintiff.
February 24, 2006	Montana and Maine file a friend-of-the-court brief supporting the four states' lawsuit.
March 6, 2006	North Carolina petitions for protection of all its roadless areas.
April 19, 2006	South Carolina petitions for protection of all its roadless areas.
May 31, 2006	New Mexico petitions for protection of all its roadless areas.
July 12, 2006	California petitions for protection of all its roadless areas.
August 11, 2006	North Dakota roadless lawsuit is settled.
September 20, 2006	Judge Elizabeth Laporte of the U.S. District Court for Northern California rules that the state petition rule was illegally adopted and the 2001 Roadless Rule, illegally repealed. She reinstates the 2001 rule nationwide, except in the Tongass National Forest.

September 20, 2006	Idaho submits a petition calling for opening most of its roadless areas to development, but Governor Risch changes his tune when he makes his oral presentation to the Roadless Area Conservation National Advisory Committee.
September 22, 2006	Wyoming asks Judge Brimmer to reinstate his previous injunction.
November 13, 2006	Colorado submits a petition outlining recommendations for managing roadless areas within its borders.
November 29, 2006	Judge Laporte issues an injunction barring road construction in connection with more than three hundred oil and gas leases sold since January 2001.
November 29, 2006	Idaho Governor Risch tells the Roadless Area Conservation Advisory Committee that, contrary to what his petition seems to say, he is seeking protection for all but 500,000 acres of its roadless areas.
February 6, 2007	Judge Laporte issues a final injunction barring the Forest Service from doing anything contrary to the 2001 Roadless Rule, except on the Tongass National Forest in Alaska.
April 9, 2007	Forest Service and the timber industry appeal Judge Laporte's decision.
April 11, 2007	New Colorado Governor Bill Ritter submits a revised petition that includes exemptions for ski areas, grazing, and coal mining.
June 7, 2007	Judge Brimmer denies Wyoming's request to reinstate his 2003 injunction.
July 5, 2007	The Tenth Circuit Court of Appeals denies the State of Wyoming's request to reopen the appeal of Judge Brimmer's injunction.
October 19, 2007	Judge Brimmer hears oral argument on Wyoming's renewed challenge to the Roadless Rule.
August 12, 2008	Judge Brimmer issues a nationwide injunction blocking the effect of the 2001 Roadless Rule, in evident contravention to Judge LaPorte's 2006 injunction.

August 13, 2008   Environmental intervenors file a notice of appeal with the
                         Tenth Circuit announcing that they will appeal Judge Brimmer's
                         injunction.

Source: Drawn from timelines compiled by The Wilderness Society, the Heritage Forests Campaign, Earthjustice, and the USDA Forest Service.

Appendix 3

Case Citations and Statutes

RARE: *Wyoming Outdoor Council v. Earl L. Butz,* 359 F. Supp. 1178 (D. Wyo. 1972); 484 F.2d 1244 (10th Cir. 1973).

Clear-cutting outlawed: *Izaak Walton League v. Earl L. Butz,* 353 F. Supp. 698 (D. Minn. 1973); 497 F.2d 849 (8th Cir. 1974).

RARE II: *California v. Block,* 483 F. Supp. 465 (E. D. Calif. 1980); 690 F.2d 753 (9th Cir. 1982).

Idaho challenges the Roadless Rule: *Kootenai Tribe of Idaho v. Veneman,* 142 F. Supp. 2d 1231 (D. Idaho 2001); 313 F.3d 1094 (9th Cir. 2002).

Wyoming challenges the Roadless Rule I: *Wyoming v. USDA,* 277 F. Supp. 2d 1197 (D. Wyo. 2003); 414 F.3d 1207 (10th Cir. 2005).

Wyoming challenges to the Roadless Rule II: *Wyoming v. USDA,* 570 F. Supp. 2d 1309 (D. Wyo. 2008).

Administrative Procedure Act: U.S. Code 5, sec. 701–706 (1946).

Endangered Species Act: U.S. Code 16, sec. 1531–1544 (1973).

Multiple-Use Sustained-Yield Act: U.S. Code 16, sec. 528–531 (1960).

National Environmental Policy Act: U. S. Code 43, sec. 4321–4370 (1970).

National Forest Management Act: U.S. Code 16, sec. 1600–1614 (1976).

Organic Administration Act: U.S. Code 16, sec. 551 (1897).

Wilderness Act: U.S. Code 16, sec. 1131–1136 (1964).

Appendix 4

Glossary

amicus curiae. Organizations or individuals who are not plaintiffs, defendants, or intervenors in a lawsuit may submit **amicus curiae** briefs to the court to make sure that their interests are considered.

appellate court. See **court of appeals.**

Article III (Three) judges. Federal judges at the district, appellate, and Supreme Court levels appointed by the president and confirmed by the Senate, as outlined in Article III of the U.S. Constitution. Such judges serve for life unless they resign or are removed for various kinds of transgressions.

Blue Ribbon Coalition. An organization that promotes access to federal and state lands for off-highway vehicles including snowmobiles, dune buggies, and all-terrain vehicles. Heavily supported by the manufacturers of snowmobiles and other such machines.

Bureau of Land Management (BLM). Agency within the Department of the Interior that manages mostly unforested lands, mostly in the West and Alaska. An exception is in Oregon, where the BLM manages heavily forested areas on the west side of the Cascade Mountains.

carbon sequestration. The capture and storage of carbon that would otherwise be emitted to the atmosphere in the process of, for example, coal combustion, and contribute to climate disruption.

clear-cut. Logging technique in which virtually all trees are felled and transported to the sawmill or the pulp mill.

comity. In a legal context, respect for and deference to one court by another when considering similar matters and issues.

cooperating agencies. In assessing the likely environmental impact of proposed projects, federal agencies can seek the assistance of states, tribes, or various other entities.

court of appeals. There are thirteen courts of appeals—eleven numbered ones that serve geographical areas, plus one for the District of Columbia and one for the Federal Circuit. The latter court was created in 1982 by the merger of federal courts that hear cases involving patents, customs, and claims.

ecosystem services. What nature provides free to humans—air to breathe, water to drink, food to eat, and so forth.

en banc. Appeals of district court rulings are first heard by three-judge panels of the appropriate circuit court of appeals. On fairly rare occasions, the subsequent appellate ruling will be reviewed by all the judges of the appeals court sitting **en banc** (this is not true of the Ninth Circuit, which has too many judges for that to be workable. A panel of eleven judges will sit in an **en banc** review in the Ninth Circuit).

environmental impact statement (EIS). An assessment of the likely environmental impact of projects federal agencies undertake themselves, provide funds for, or grant permits for. Required by the National Environmental Policy Act of 1970.

Federal Register Daily publication of the federal government where new rules and regulations first appear.

Forest Roads Working Group. Coalition of organizations seeking common ground in various approaches to managing roadless areas on the national forests.

friend of the court. See **amicus curiae.**

ghost roads. Roads that are carved by Jeeps and other kinds of off-road vehicles.

injunction. An order from a court that blocks an action by an individual or an agency; an order that requires an individual or agency to carry out a given action. Injunctions can be preliminary or permanent.

intervene. To join a suit as a party on the side of either the plaintiff or the defendant. There are two kinds of intervention: **permissive** intervention, which is at the discretion of the judge; and intervention **as of right,** wherein parties that can show a certain vital interest in the case may intervene automatically, without permission from a judge.

intervenor. Person or organization that joins a lawsuit in progress on the side of either the **plaintiff** or the **defendant.**

inventoried roadless areas (IRAS). Generally unroaded areas on the national forests, 5,000 acres or larger and not already protected as wilderness. Inventories were carried out in the 1970s in the RARE process, the Roadless Area Review and Evaluations.

Lieberman report. A report by the majority staff of the Senate Committee on Government Affairs that analyzed actions by the Bush administration in early 2001, which sought to delay or undo three rules, including the Roadless Rule, promulgated by the Clinton administration.

magistrate. A judge appointed by a federal court to hear cases and render suggested decisions. Magistrates are not confirmed by the Senate and are not appointed for life.

memorandum of understanding (MOU). A written agreement between agencies, or between states and agencies, that outlines common understandings of a project to be undertaken.

Ninth Circuit Court of Appeals. Hears appeals of federal district court rulings from Alaska, Hawaii, California, Arizona, Nevada, Oregon, Washington, Idaho, Montana, Guam, and the Northern Marianas Islands. Headquartered in San Francisco.

not-for-profit (nonprofit). An organization whose purpose is something other than making money. Not-for-profits have no shareholders and are generally governed by a board of directors or trustees.

Outdoor Industry Association (OIA). An organization of equipment manufacturers and retailers, outfitters, and others catering to hikers, backpackers, river runners, and the like.

plaintiff/defendant. A **plaintiff** is the initiator of a lawsuit and seeks to change or stop the action of the **defendant**, who is alleged to be violating one or more laws or rules.

purchaser road credit. A system whereby a timber company may deduct the cost of building logging roads from the amount it bids to pay the Forest Service for a timber sale, now called a **specified road credit.**

RARE. The first Roadless Area Review and Evaluation carried out pursuant to the Wilderness Act of 1964.

RARE II. The second Roadless Area Review and Evaluation, carried out in the late 1970s when the first review was found to be inadequate upon review by the Forest Service, after complaints from the public. Major parts of **RARE II** were found inadequate later by a federal judge.

Roadless Area Conservation National Advisory Committee (RACNAC). Committee created by the Forest Service in 2005 to review state petitions concerning management of roadless areas on the national forests.

Sagebrush Rebellion. A movement from the 1970s that sought to have federal lands in the West given to the states.

sustained yield. An approach to silviculture using the principle that no more wood should be harvested from a forest during a given period than will be replaced by growth.

Tenth Circuit Court of Appeals. Hears appeals of federal district court rulings from Colorado, Wyoming, Oklahoma, New Mexico, Utah, and Kansas, plus parts of Yellowstone National Park that extend into Montana and Idaho. Headquartered in Denver.

vacatur. Order from a higher court to a lower court to wipe away the lower court's decision, opinion, or order in a given matter.

wilderness study areas (wsas). Areas of Bureau of Land Management lands that have been proposed for protection as wilderness.

zero-cut policy. A position some environmental organizations have taken, opposing all commercial logging on the national forests.

Bibliography

Baldwin, Pamela, and Ross Gorte. *The National Forest System Roadless Areas Initiative*. Congressional Research Service, updated September 7, 2006.

Best, Constance, and Laurie A. Wayburn. *America's Forest Trust: Status and Stewardship*. Island Press, 2001.

Brooks, Paul. *Roadless Area*. Alfred A. Knopf, 1942.

Center for Biological Diversity. *Wild at Heart: Saving the Last of America's Roadless Backcountry*. 2008.

Dombeck, Michael P., Christopher A. Wood, and Jack E. Williams. *From Conquest to Conservation: Our Public Lands Legacy*. Island Press, 2003.

Durbin, Kathie. *Tongass: Pulp Politics and the Fight for the Alaska Rainforest*. Oregon State University Press, 1999.

———. *Tree Huggers: Victory, Defeat and Renewal in the Northwest Ancient Forest Campaign*. Mountaineers, 1996.

Frome, Michael. *Battle for the Wilderness*. University of Utah Press, 1974.

———. *The Forest Service*. Perseus Books, 1984.

Furnish, Jim. *Eastern Roadless Areas Under Threat: How the U.S. Forest Service Minimizes Roadless Areas with Biased Procedures*. Heritage Forests Campaign, 2004.

Glicksman, Robert L. "Traveling in Opposite Directions: Roadless Area Management Under the Clinton and Bush Administrations." *Environmental Law* (2004): 101–165.

Goldfuss, Christina. *Worth More Wild: The Value of Pennsylvania's Roadless National Forest*. Environment Pennsylvania Research and Policy Center, 2007.

Havlick, David G. "Behind the Wheel: A Look Back at Public Land Roads." *Forest History Today*, Spring (2002): 10-20.

———. *No Place Distant: Roads and Motorized Recreation on America's Public Lands.* Island Press, 2002.

Hirt, Paul W. *A Conspiracy of Optimism: Management of the National Forests since World War Two.* University of Nebraska Press, 1994.

Ketchum, Robert Glenn, and Carey D. Ketchum. *The Tongass: Alaska's Vanishing Rain Forest.* Aperture, 1987.

Kirk, Ruth, ed. *The Enduring Forests.* Mountaineers, 1996.

Krieger, Douglas J. *Economic Value of Forest Ecosystem Services: A Review.* The Wilderness Society, n.d.

Loomis, John B., and Robert Richardson. *Economic Values of Protecting Roadless Areas in the United States.* The Wilderness Society and Heritage Forests Campaign, 2000.

Lorah, Paul, and Rob Southwick. *Historical Economic Performance of Oregon and Western Counties Associated with Roadless and Wilderness Areas.* Southwick Associates, 2000.

Marsh, Kevin R. *Drawing Lines in the Forest: Creating Wilderness Areas in the Pacific Northwest.* University of Washington Press, 2007.

Nappier, Sharon. *Lost in the Forest: How the Forest Service's Misdirection, Mismanagement, and Mischief Squanders Your Tax Dollars.* Taxpayers for Common Sense, 2002.

National Environmental Trust and Heritage Forests Campaign. *Protecting America's National Forests: Saving the Last Wild 30%.* N.d.

Petersen, Thomas Reed, ed. *A Road Runs Through It: Reviving Wild Places.* Johnson Books, 2006.

Scott, Doug. *The Enduring Wilderness: Protecting Our Natural Heritage Through the Wilderness Act.* Fulcrum Publishing, 2004.

Servid, Carolyn, and Donald Snow, eds. *The Book of the Tongass.* Milkweed Editions, 1999.

Shoaf, Bill. *The Taking of the Tongass: Alaska's Rainforest.* Running Wolf Press, 2000.

Stritholt, James R., and Dominick A. DellaSala. "Importance of Roadless Areas in Biodiversity Conservation in Forested Ecosystems: Case Study of the Klamath-Siskiyou Ecoregion of the United States." *Conservation Biology*, December (2001): 1742-1754.

Thomas, Jack Ward. *The Journals of a Forest Service Chief*. Edited by Harold K. Steen. Forest History Society in association with the University of Washington Press, 2004.

Turner, James Morton. "Conservation Science and Forest Service Policy for Roadless Areas." *Conservation Biology* 20 (2006): 713-722.

Turner, Tom. "Unsettling Developments." *Environmental Forum*, January–February (2004): 32–41.

Weurthner, George, ed. *Thrillcraft: The Environmental Consequences of Motorized Recreation*. Foundation for Deep Ecology, 2007.

Wilkinson, Todd. *Science Under Siege: The Politicians' War on Nature and Truth*. Johnson Books, 1998.

Zakin, Susan. *Coyotes and Town Dogs: Earth First! and the Environmental Movement*. Viking, 1993.

Index